D1758702

University Centre at
Blackburn
College

Telephone: 01254 292165

Please return this book on or before the last date shown

CENTRALISATION, DEVOLUTION AND THE FUTURE OF LOCAL GOVERNMENT IN ENGLAND

English local government is in a state of decline after 40 years of incremental but cumulative centralisation by central government.

This book is the first to directly address this trend's impact upon the institution of local government, a crucial element in the democratic viability of a unitary state. The process of centralisation, and its corrosive effect on the status and responsibilities of local government, have been widely recognised and deplored among politicians and senior officers within local government, and by academics with an interest in this field. However, there has been no study exploring in detail its impact, and, equally important, suggesting ways in which the growing imbalance between the powers of central and local government should be rectified. This book fills this gap.

This text will be of key interest to scholars, students and practitioners of local government, and more generally to those interested in what has been happening to British politics and governance.

Steve Leach worked at the Institute of Local Government Studies (INLOGOV) from 1977 to 1996, by which time he held the position of Reader. He was then appointed Professor of Local Government at De Montfort University, UK, a position he held until his retirement in 2009, and still holds on an Emeritus basis.

John Stewart joined the Institute of Local Government Studies (INLOGOV) at the University of Birmingham, UK, in 1966, and became Professor of Local Government in the early 1970s, a position he held until he retired in the late 1990s, and now holds on an Emeritus basis. He was a member of the Layfield committee on Local Government Finance (1974–1976), and has contributed to many other government inquiries.

George Jones joined the London School of Economics (LSE) in 1966 and was appointed Professor of Government in 1976, a position he held until his retirement in 2007 and which he later held on an Emeritus basis. He, too, was a member of the Layfield Committee and gave evidence to a range of other government inquiries.

ROUTLEDGE STUDIES IN BRITISH POLITICS

Series editors: *Patrick Diamond and Tim Bale of Queen Mary University of London (QMUL), UK.*

This series aims to promote research excellence in political science, political history and public-policy making, whilst addressing a wide array of political dynamics, contexts, histories and ideas. It will retain a particular focus on British government, British politics and public policy, while locating those issues within a European and global context.

1. Centralisation, Devolution and the Future of Local Government in England
Steve Leach, John Stewart and George Jones

CENTRALISATION, DEVOLUTION AND THE FUTURE OF LOCAL GOVERNMENT IN ENGLAND

Steve Leach, John Stewart and George Jones

Routledge
Taylor & Francis Group

LONDON AND NEW YORK

First published 2018
by Routledge
2 Park Square, Milton Park, Abingdon, Oxon OX14 4RN

and by Routledge
711 Third Avenue, New York, NY 10017

Routledge is an imprint of the Taylor & Francis Group, an informa business

© 2018 Steve Leach, John Stewart and George Jones

The right of Steve Leach, John Stewart and George Jones to be
identified as authors of this work has been asserted by them in
accordance with sections 77 and 78 of the Copyright, Designs and
Patents Act 1988.

All rights reserved. No part of this book may be reprinted or reproduced
or utilised in any form or by any electronic, mechanical, or other means,
now known or hereafter invented, including photocopying and
recording, or in any information storage or retrieval system, without
permission in writing from the publishers.

Trademark notice: Product or corporate names may be trademarks or
registered trademarks, and are used only for identification and
explanation without intent to infringe.

British Library Cataloguing in Publication Data
A catalogue record for this book is available from the British Library

Library of Congress Cataloging in Publication Data
Names: Leach, Steve, 1942- author. | Stewart, John David, 1929-
author. | Jones, G. W. (George William), author.
Title: Centralisation, devolution and the future of local government in
England / Steve Leach, John Stewart and George Jones.
Other titles: Centralization, devolution and the future of local
government in England
Description: Abingdon, Oxon ; New York, NY : Routledge, 2017. |
Series: Routledge studies in British politics ; 1 | Includes bibliographical
references and index.
Identifiers: LCCN 2016059006 | ISBN 9781138222373 (hardback) |
ISBN 9781138222380 (paperback) | ISBN 9781315407944 (ebook)
Subjects: LCSH: Local government--England. | Central-local
government relations--England. | Decentralization in government--
England.
Classification: LCC JS3111 .L424 2017 | DDC 320.80942 dc23
LC record available at https://lccn.loc.gov/2

ISBN: 978-1-138-22237-3 (hbk)
ISBN: 978-1-138-22238-0 (pbk)
ISBN: 978-1-315-40794-4 (ebk)

Typeset in Bembo
by Taylor & Francis Books

MIX
Paper from
responsible sour
FSC™ C0139

BLACKBURN COLLEGE LIBRARY

BB 67040	
Askews & Holts	26-Oct-2017
UCL320.8094 LEA	

Professor George Jones, our colleague and fellow author, died suddenly and unexpectedly on 6 April 2017, a short time after we completed this book and sent it to the publishers. He is greatly missed.

We hope the book will be seen as an expression of George's commitment to strong and effective local government and local democracy, to counteract the dangers of excessive centralisation. This commitment has been a dominant feature of his work throughout his long and distinguished academic career.

We both feel privileged to have been George's partners in the writing of this book and hope it will be viewed as a tribute to George and to his work with and for local government.

Steve Leach and John Stewart

CONTENTS

ACKNOWLEDGEMENTS

Steve Leach would like to thank the following people for their contributions to this book. Professor Colin Copus and Mark Roberts, colleagues at De Montfort University, were both involved in an earlier joint venture to produce a book covering similar ground to this one. The lively discussions have influenced his thinking about the past and future of local government in England. In particular, Mark Roberts's ideas and publications on 'narrative theory' have significantly influenced the content of Chapter 4, while Colin Copus's thoughts and publications on local government structure and reorganisations have had a similarly substantive influence on the content of Chapter 8. Dennis Reed, former chief executive of the Local Government Information Unit, made significant contributions to the author's thinking about electoral systems (Chapter 7) and provided an invaluable critique of an earlier version of Chapter 6, which deals with local government finance. In addition, their joint articles for *Municipal Journal* on the devolution agenda and the Northern Powerhouse initiative form the basis of much of Chapter 9. Former Chief Planning Officers John Dean and Martin Bradshaw provided helpful input to the discussion of changes in town planning in Chapters 3 and 4. Councillor Peter Downes provided numerous insights on the impact of the recent move to academies and free schools (see Chapter 3). Professor Tony Travers, a renowned expert on local government finance, kindly read through the draft chapter on this topic, and made many helpful suggestions for strengthening it.

All the authors are grateful to Andrew Taylor of Taylor & Francis for responding positively to their initial proposal, putting it out to referees and then agreeing to publish it, and to Sophie Iddamalgoda, their main reference point throughout the process, for her unfailing helpfulness and patience as a series of deadlines were missed. They would like to thank their wives – Karen Lloyd, Diana Jones and Theresa Stewart – for their patience and support, and to assure them that this is almost certainly the last venture of this nature they will be embarking upon.

Sole responsibility for the contents of this book rests of course with its three authors.

INTRODUCTION

The plight of local government and central–local relationships

From 1964 to 1971, one of the authors was a practising town planner, first in Manchester City Council and then in Cheshire County Council. At that time, the world of local government was in a very different state from the marginalised and emasculated condition in which it finds itself in 2017.

Five main differences are striking. First, 50 years ago, relations between central and local government were cordial and uncontroversial. In the huge challenge of post-war reconstruction, local authorities had demonstrated their capacity to deliver on priorities typically shared with the centre. They had constructed millions of council houses, cleared vast tracts of unfit housing, redeveloped town centres, and implemented road schemes that sought to segregate vehicles from pedestrians. They had organised the move to the post-war tripartite model of secondary education (and later to the comprehensive system) and were shortly to introduce an integrated model of social-services provision. With the benefit of hindsight, some mistakes were made, such as the commitment to high-rise flats (although they were largely at the behest of central government). But, in the main, local government proved to be an effective agency for the delivery of services and projects of regeneration, operating in a mutually beneficial partnership with central government.

Second, local authorities were congruent with places with which local people identified. For example, to the east of Manchester, in what is now Tameside, there exists a conglomeration of small towns, each with their own distinctive characteristics and fierce local loyalties. In 1965 these towns operated under a local-government system in which their identities were recognised, with separate authorities for Ashton-under-Lyne, Hyde, Stalybridge, Mossley, Audenshaw, and Dukinfield among others. It was not as localised as the French system of communes, but it was a reasonably close approximation.

Third, council leaders (and other leading local politicians) often became MPs, and, sometimes, in due course, cabinet ministers. Their experience of running councils was seen as a valuable asset by constituency party selection panels. Going back to the immediate post-war period, Clement Attlee, Herbert Morrison, Nye Bevan, and Ellen Wilkinson had all served apprenticeships in local councils. That tradition was still going strong in 1965, and indeed continued for some time thereafter (the names of John Major, David Blunkett, Edwina Curry, Gillian Shepherd, and Stephen Byers spring to mind).

Fourth, the value of medium-/long-term planning was widely recognised and accepted, almost as much so as its neo-liberal market-driven antithesis is today. This positive attitude was particularly true of town and country planning, for which the 1960s and 1970s was its heyday. At national level, economic planning was also in favour. In local authorities corporate planning, which involved the setting of strategies for the future of a wide range of council services within the framework of an overall vision for the area, was beginning to emerge by the mid-1970s.

Fifth, there was considerable variation in the policies and in the expenditure plans of different authorities. Typically, Labour councils wanted to spend more than their Conservative counterparts, reflecting a concern with social justice, and positive discrimination in favour of the less-well-off. At that time there existed in local government the capacity for such choices, with local electorates able to demonstrate their support for or opposition to both high-spending and low-spending administrations at subsequent local elections.

In general, during the 1960s, local authorities operated as change agents, with central government providing enabling legislation, financial incentives, and resources, although at that time councils were much less reliant on central grant than they are now, and advice was typically disseminated through departmental circulars. Local government bore the primary responsibility for planning and delivering services, and for development work in town centres, new municipal housing estates and transportation networks, with the rating system (including business rates) giving local authorities considerable freedom in budget-setting. The relationship between central and local government was often described as a 'partnership'. There was little of the tension and conflict which have permeated the relationship from the 1980s onwards. The centre relied on local government to implement changes that it wished to see introduced (the perceived need for which was usually shared between the two levels), and local government was typically content to work within the (often flexible) policy parameters outlined by the centre. At the time it was difficult to see how the relationship might be different, or, indeed, why it would ever need to be.

All has changed. Central–local relations have deteriorated, a process that began under Margaret Thatcher, and recently reached its nadir in a secretary of state (Eric Pickles) who claimed that he 'enjoyed bashing local government'. Many of the smaller authorities that represented real communities disappeared in the 1974 reorganisation to be replaced by non-place councils such as Sefton, Kirklees, Trafford, Tendring and Havering, whose locations must be a total mystery even to many of those familiar with the geography of England. The process of separating authorities from real places has continued in a series of increasingly bizarre reorganisations, the most recent of which created large, all-purpose counties such as Northumberland and Cornwall, where the 'local' dimension of local government has now disappeared completely. The recruitment of MPs from positions of local leadership has declined, in favour of a surge in the numbers of 'career politicians', with no experience of local government, nor indeed any kind of paid work outside the cloisters of Westminster. The value of medium-term planning for land-use issues, the location of economic development or comprehensive local strategies, all of which seemed 'common sense' in the 1960s and 1970s, has fallen into abeyance. Many of the powers enjoyed by local government in the 1960s have been withdrawn or drastically curtailed or circumscribed. The scope for council-house construction has virtually disappeared, and most council estates are now managed by 'arms-length' bodies. The role of councils in education has been marginalised, not least by the exponential growth of academies and free schools, both funded directly by the centre. Many elements of social and environmental services have, under government pressure or requirement, been outsourced, leaving local authorities increasingly reliant on the practices and priorities of private contractors. The capacity for strategic land-use planning, reflecting genuinely local priorities, has been greatly diluted. And the scope for local choice, either over levels of local expenditure or over local policy has been drastically reduced, largely through a system of local-government finance that leaves little freedom for local choice, and through a growth in central prescription and control, seen as required by those working within a centralist culture. Enabling legislation has been increasingly replaced by an almost endless stream of detailed secondary legislation and reams of detailed guidance.

To record these changes, which add up to a major and continuing increase in centralisation, and a concomitant cumulative decline in the role, responsibilities, and status of local government, should not be taken to imply that local government during the 1960s and 1970s was without its faults. It made misjudgements about the social acceptability of high-rise flats and urban ring-roads, although in both cases with the support of central government. Its Direct Labour Organisations were often inefficient, but restrictive practices amongst trade unions were as widespread at the time in the private sector as the public sector. And all public (and indeed private sector) organisations are prone to mistakes and performance failures from time to time, including central government itself (see King and Crewe 2014). In what can be seen as a growing crisis in the democratic viability of our unitary state, it is important to explore what lies behind this contrast between the state of local government (and of central–local relations) in 1965 and 2017 respectively, and to examine what should be done about it.

How can we explain this contrast? Chapter 4 argues that the concept of disjointed incrementalism (see Lindblom 1959), linked to a changing set of attitudes (and assumptive worlds) in Westminster and Whitehall provides a more convincing explanation than a long-term centralist conspiracy to undermine local government. But while there is no conscious conspiracy, there is a centralist culture, within which centralisation is seen as the natural response to public concerns and media pressures. What should be emphasised is the present-day outcome of what has happened over this 50-year period: the current marginalised role of local government within the democratic state. This outcome is something about which we should be greatly concerned, however it has transpired. So why isn't the plight of local government higher on the public agenda?

If Parliament now has a public-image problem, reflecting people's increasing mistrust of MPs (accentuated, but not caused, by the expenses scandal in 2009) and the disillusionment with all the traditional parties (illustrated by the low proportion of votes gained by the traditional parties in the 2015 general election), the problem for local government is different. Surveys show that local government as an institution and councillors collectively inspire greater levels of public trust than do Parliament and MPs (Wilson and Game 2011). But local government does not generate anything like the intensity of interest and emotion that national government does. There is a climate of indifference about it, except at the personal level, when individuals feel angered about the impact of particular local decisions. There has been no rush to the barricades to protest about the way in which local council budgets have been drastically and disproportionately cut, compared with other public sector agencies such as the National Health Service (NHS), as part of the government's economic strategy (which is itself open to criticism). It was not always so; the public opposition to the introduction of the poll tax, and to the politically inspired abolition of the Greater London Council (GLC) both took place within the last 30 years. But at present there is little sign of public concern about the present emasculated state of local government.

While the authors of this book are deeply concerned about the undermining of the role of local government and of the diminishing vitality of local democracy, we are also concerned about its impact on central government itself. The growth in centralisation has created major problems for the workings of central government departments, through overloading their responsibilities, as they become ever more deeply involved in local affairs, as a result of detailed prescription of what local authorities (and other local public agencies) should do and how they should do it, leading to enhanced scrutiny and control procedures. These developments have exposed the consequences for central government in seeking detailed involvement, when they are not directly involved in the problems faced at local level, nor in the actions taken to meet those problems. Too often it is government from a distance, reflecting an ignorance of the diversity of local circumstances. Centralisation, as documented in this book, has become increasingly ineffective, and has resulted in a failing national system of government, which attempts to exert too much central control of local matters, without having adequate understanding of the local context in which they are intervening.

The current state of local government and its uncertain future should be recognised as matters of great significance to everyone who is worried about the health and credibility of our democratic system in Britain, but particularly within England. It is indisputable that over the past 30 to 40 years there has been a profound shift in the balance of power between the central and local state. We are currently living in one of the most centralised states in Western Europe, not as the result of a deliberate strategy by one particular government to achieve this goal, but rather as the result of the cumulative erosion of local government's powers by a succession of different governments responding within the dominant centralist culture, which sees such centralisation as the natural response. This development should be a matter of great national concern. But for the reasons mentioned earlier, it isn't. In the centre's justification of the need for austerity in local government, economic arguments have dominated. Concerns about the impact of austerity-linked centralisation measures on the democratic health of the nation, in which local government is a major player, have received much less attention. It is time that this imbalance was recognised and rectified.

The all-party commitment to some form of devolution within England, in the aftermath of the referendum in September 2014 on Scottish independence, provided a window of opportunity to highlight this concern and respond radically to the problem. But it also posed a danger for local government. What is needed is an objective, in-depth analysis of the problems, from which can be built a robust and comprehensive set of evidence-based recommendations. In the run-up to the May 2015 general election, however, Chancellor George Osborne set in motion an ad-hoc form of devolution, known as the Northern Powerhouse, which involved the allocation of previously centrally-controlled budgets for services such as passenger transport and economic development to the Combined Authorities of Greater Manchester, West Midlands, South Yorkshire, Tees Valley, the Liverpool City Region and the North-East Region, with indications that this initiative would be extended to other areas (see Chapter 9). Welcome though this rare example of devolution by the coalition was perceived to be (at least by the authorities involved), it should not be allowed to pre-empt a more considered analysis of devolution options designed to ensure the enhancement of local choice, which is, in fact, diminished by some aspects of the current proposals (for example, the imposition of elected mayors). It would indeed be a wasted opportunity if this kind of ad-hoc interventionism (possibly inspired by considerations of electoral advantage) were to set the tone for the way in which devolution is subsequently dealt with.

This book is in effect a political polemic from three academics who have previously published, singly or jointly, a series of academic books and articles which sought to comply with the familiar expectations of such texts: balance, objectivity, and referencing. The book differs from their previous scholarly publications. It is an unashamedly polemical piece of writing which draws attention to what we see as a crisis in the only other directly elected institution of government that exists outside Westminster, and hence in the overall national system of government, and which sets out a series of proposals for rectifying the current imbalance in power between the two levels. In fact, it would be difficult to undertake a balanced appraisal of the arguments justifying the long-term drift to greater centralisation and those critical of this process, because there has been a notable absence of the former. The process has cumulatively developed without anyone owning, justifying, or taking responsibility for it. Rather, we can discern the development of a set of tacit centralist assumptions about the respective roles of the central and local states, which should be much more strongly contested than they have been, an omission which this book sets out to rectify. Although drawing heavily on the published work of the three authors, it also, where appropriate, highlights the work of other writers who have been prepared to challenge these assumptions, as the process of centralisation has gathered momentum, for example, Simon Jenkins and Tony Travers.

The book is in two parts. The first part looks back at the history of local government and seeks to understand why its status has declined so markedly over the past 50 years. The first chapter sets out the case for a system of local government which has a genuinely governmental capacity, that is, the ability to make democratic local policy choices which reflect local circumstances coupled with the ability to raise adequate local resources to finance them. Until the early 1980s, this case was largely taken for granted, but has since then faded into the background. It is important to remind ourselves of how vital the local government's role is in a unitary state such as Britain.

The second chapter identifies five successive periods in the development of local government, revealing their distinctive characteristics, and drawing lessons which will be of value to those seeking to strengthen local government at the present time. The last of these periods covers the 13 years of Labour government between 1997 and 2010, and Chapter 3, which follows, is devoted to an analysis of the attitude of the 2010–2015 coalition government to local government, and the impact of the measures that it introduced, notably the 2011 Localism Act. The title of the chapter, 'The Myth of Localism', gives a clear indication of our verdict! Chapter 4 explains the cumulative process of centralisation since 1980, in which governments of varying political colours have all played a part. While it focuses on the concept of disjointed incrementalism, operating within the assumptions of the centralist culture, it also highlights the effect of centralisation on central government itself, creating an overloaded central system, unable to draw upon direct contact with or a detailed understanding of the reality of issues and concerns at local level.

The second part of the book moves forward from our analysis of what has gone wrong over the past 40 years or so and outlines some proposals to restore the governmental capacity of local authorities, building up its role and redressing the imbalance between central and local responsibilities which has developed over this period. Successive chapters (5–8) deal with strengthening the constitutional position of local government, providing a buoyant resource base to enable it to make real local choices, equipping it with a set of democratic and political-management qualities which would strengthen its legitimacy, and developing a coherent response to the chaotic territorial structure of local government which has resulted from a series of ad-hoc reorganisations from 1986 onwards. Chapter 9 explores the so-called devolution policy, introduced in 2014 by George Osborne in the form of the 'Northern Powerhouse' initiative, and then extended after the 2015 election to a range of non-metropolitan areas. This policy is currently one which dominates the pages of the local government press, and has profound, although as yet unclear, implications for local government. The final Reflections and Conclusions chapter summarises our proposals for transforming local government which were developed in Chapters 5–8, and considers the prospects of their being adopted in the post-Brexit world which now faces us.

Any book which seeks to document the declining role of local government in our society, and to propose measures for reversing this trend, will necessarily focus primarily on the relationship between central and local government, because it is only through changes in the structures, processes, and (most important) attitudes of the former that real progress can be made, not just in the role and working of local authorities, but in the working of central government itself. Local government has a crucial role to play in a process of real (as opposed to partial and conditional) devolution, but it cannot do so in the absence of a fundamental reappraisal from the centre of its attitude to local government. In the final chapter, the main barriers to this desired outcome, all of which have been identified in the earlier chapters, and which are apparent in the current stance of the centre towards local government, are listed, together with the measures necessary to overcome them.

In summary the book can be seen as emerging from a profound sense of anger by three academics about what has happened to a democratic institution, which has served the country well in the past, but which now appears to be in terminal decline, creating in turn a failing national governmental system. A challenge to centralisation, as set out in this book, could pave the way for a revitalised system of genuine local government, operating in conjunction with flourishing institutions of local democracy, an outcome which is sorely needed.

PART I
The current situation

1

THE JUSTIFICATION FOR LOCAL GOVERNMENT

Throughout its history, the value of having a strong local government system in England, with the ability to make local choices that affect the quality of life of local residents, to whom local authorities are accountable through periodic local elections, has been widely accepted, indeed, for the most part unquestioned. It is a view that the authors of this book whole-heartedly endorse. However, over the past 35 years, this value has come to be questioned, not by local residents, but by successive governments who have taken a series of measures to reduce its powers and diminish its status. It has become important to remind ourselves why local government is so important an element in the government of our nation, in a way which 40 years ago would not have been necessary. This aim forms the focus of this chapter.

At times, the cavalier attitude to local government adopted by the coalition government of 2010–2015, and in particular by Eric Pickles, the secretary of state with responsibility for it, leads one to wonder whether there is an emergent view in Westminster, shared by (some) ministers and senior civil servants, that it might be better if local government were dispensed with altogether! It is hard to imagine a democratic state without a significant level of governmental responsibility at a sub-national level, and there is no Western democracy that has taken this unprecedented step. But we cannot just assume that some form of local government is necessary. To develop a case for a strong system of local government with significant devolved powers, it is necessary to work our way through a series of basic questions about its role and the appropriate scope of its responsibilities, starting with the most fundamental question: do we need local government at all?

A local government-free state?

Can a persuasive 'in principle' case be made for dispensing with local government altogether? In its absence, there would necessarily have to be some system for the local administration of centrally prescribed services (as is currently the case with Job Centre Plus). But this kind of local administration is not local government. Local government requires a capacity for exercising local choice (which may be subject in certain circumstances to central government constraint), and a mechanism by which it can be held accountable for the choices made at the local level. To some extent appointed bodies such as the former health Primary Care Trusts (PCTs) met the first criterion, but they did not meet the second.

What would be the arguments against the centre taking formal responsibility for the entire range of services and functions currently allocated to local authorities? What would be the problem if groups of locality-based civil servants (or other unelected appointees), operating from sub-national offices, were to administer education, social services, refuse collection, and land-use planning in line with centrally specified rules over admissions criteria for schools, frequency of refuse collection, and allocation of social housing? It would certainly be possible to organise local decision-making in this way. But could it ever be justified?

There are five reasons why, in the total absence of some kind of local government system, local administration by appointed officials, on a service-by-service basis, would inevitably prove a vastly inferior alternative.

First, it would struggle to recognise and respond to the *diversity of local circumstances*, traditions, and preferences that are to be found amongst our cities, towns, and counties. There are significant differences between the socio-economic profiles of affluent suburban authorities such as Richmond-on-Thames, decaying seaside resorts like Hastings, traditional cities struggling to reinvent themselves, such as Stoke-on-Trent, and new-town based authorities like Telford and Wrekin. All these places have their distinctive histories, culture, and priorities, which can be recognised, understood, and responded to by a democratic politically led institution, in a way that local administration could not hope to replicate.

Second, local administration would inevitably lack the *capacity to respond to the public protest* that would inevitably develop over issues such as how central rules were applied in contentious planning applications, closures of schools, or elderly persons homes, and loss of funding experienced by arts/cultural organisations. It would be limited in its ability to respond, because it would lack the capacity for local choice, and a mechanism for local accountability.

Third, there would be a *lack of capacity to prioritise local services* (which is always necessary, and becomes particularly challenging at times of financial constraint) *or to join them up* to realise potential synergies amongst them. To develop this kind of capacity would require some form of integration of the various service agencies concerned into a collective mechanism: either a partnership (but how could a partnership be expected to make the difficult prioritisation decisions required?), or something which would resemble a multi-purpose local authority (but how would decisions be reached and how could those taking them, in what would in effect be a complex and unwieldy QUANGO – quasi-autonomous non-governmental organisation – be held accountable?).

Fourth, an unelected body of this nature would not be accountable to local people for local choices, since national accountability through ministers could never reflect nor respond to local views. Finally, it would further overburden an already overstretched and flawed system of national government and national accountability.

To meet these challenges of inter-service choice and service-interconnection (to achieve goals which transcend individual services) it is inevitable that there would have to be created in each locality an institution closely resembling a local authority, but it would be one which was totally dominated by outposts of central departments, without a vestige of the democratic accountability which local authorities provide.

All of the questions we have so far raised (and answered) as to why local government is needed have been premised on the assumption that the key purpose of local government is to deliver (and to co-ordinate and prioritise) local *services*. But important though the service provision role is, we would strongly dispute that that is the primary reason for the existence of local authorities. As influential thinkers such as Michael Lyons and Simon Jenkins have emphasised, the primary purpose of local government transcends the responsibility for service provision. It encompasses – or should encompass – 'community governance' – identifying and responding to the full range of local problems, challenges, aspirations, and opportunities which face the locality (see Stewart 2000). Central government does not see itself simply (or indeed primarily) as a multi-service-providing or-commissioning agency.

Neither should local authorities be seen in this way, if they are to merit the characterisation of local *government*.

Economies and diseconomies of scale

There is a further argument to address which is made by those who consider that services should be specified centrally and then administered by means of local implementation machinery. It is the familiar efficiency argument associated with 'economies of scale'. Hospital rationalisation provides one familiar example of this kind of thinking, and the ill-considered move towards large-scale 'unitary' authorities another.

The 'economies of scale' arguments are by no means conclusive. Some analysts have argued that economics of scale operate only up to a particular level (for example, of population served), after which diseconomies set in, and that there are diseconomies of scale that reflect the complexities of communication involved, which inevitably increase as scale increases.

Linked to the 'economies of scale' position is the 'disadvantages of decentralisation' (see Allen 1990) – the argument that decentralisation is more costly than centralisation, because it duplicates scarce financial resources and staff. Things can be run more cheaply from the centre, it is claimed, whether the centre is central government, or a large local authority such as Birmingham. But Wilson and Game (2011, p39) point out that Birmingham's experience challenges this assumption. The city council (England's largest local authority) has devolved significant elements of its service delivery and policy-making to neighbourhood offices and district committees. In an in-depth Overview and Scrutiny review of devolution (including its financial costs), the following conclusion was reached:

> More likely than not, a more centralised model (of service delivery) would entail higher operating costs than the current devolved structure. Savings only arose if functions were dropped.
>
> *(Birmingham City Council 2006, p43)*

But is this finding so surprising? The 1960 Royal Commission sought evidence of economies of scale, but failed to find any, and we have already noted the phenomenon of 'diseconomies of scale'. Indeed, as one Birmingham officer put it, there can also be 'economies of smallness, that can be enormous when you get local engagement and volunteering' (cited in Wilson and Game 2011, p40).

It is also important to recognise that the 'economies of scale' argument is closely linked to the service provision role of local government, and focuses on considerations of efficiency and expediency. But, as Chandler (2010) argues, there are equally important issues of ethics, moral purpose, and local integrity – long established in the history of thinking about local government – which imply different conclusions as to what should be the most appropriate roles and scales of operation of local authorities.

We also need to recognise the centralist argument about 'equality' in standards of service provision across the country, which has come to be associated with the criticisms of the 'unfairness' of the so-called 'post-code lottery' (which could equally be characterised as 'post-code choice'). We find it hard to equate an awareness of the diversity of local traditions, circum-stances, and preferences with the (intrinsically centralist) arguments in favour of uniformity in service standards and provision. However, the influence of the 'post-code lottery' is such that a fuller critical response is needed, which is provided in Chapter 5.

Accountability and representative democracy

We have argued that an appointed multi-purpose body with responsibility for local services (and local community governance) could not be 'held accountable' to local people in any meaningful sense. There are a range of different meanings attached to the term 'local accountability' but no-one has yet succeeded in identifying any accountability mechanism which would be appropriate in the above circumstances, and which does not involve citizens having opportunities to judge the performance of the elec-ted individuals and parties in their area, and their proposals and policies for the future, at regular local elections.

Much has been written about the shortcoming of local representative democracy, typically citing the low turnout at local elections, the alleged low and declining quality of local councillors (but without any evidence to justify the allegation), and the tendency of electors to vote in response to the performance of national government rather than on local issues or the qualities of local councillors and candidates, ignoring the evidence of variations in voting patterns between authorities. These assumed problems do not invalidate the principle of local representative democracy. Such problems may well have come about partly (or mainly) through the decline in powers and status of local authorities over the years (see Chapter 2).

What other possibilities are there for expressing local representative democracy? There are a whole range of operational options that can and should be considered: council size, number of tiers, frequency of election, the form of local elections (for example, first-past-the-post or some form of PR), and the nature of political leadership (including elected mayors). These various choices are explored in Chapter 7. The important point to emphasise is the link between representative democracy and accountability, and the absence of any viable alternative to it. Local representative democracy is by no means a sufficient condition for healthy local government; as we argue below it needs to be supplemented by some form of participatory democracy. But it is a necessary condition. Far from participatory democracy being seen as undermining representative democracy, it should be seen as a necessary support.

The case against 'single-purpose authorities'

Even if the arguments we have put forward about the need for an election-based system of local accountability are accepted, there remains the possibility that elections (and accountability) could be considered separately, function by function. Elections were held in 2012 for police commissioners in English counties (with pathetically low turnouts). Elections for mayoral candidates are now established in some authorities, although by no means widespread (and are in addition to, not a replacement for, council elections). In principle, it would be possible to extend this practice to hold elections for a number of commissioners with responsibility for specific services or functions (children's services, town planning, transportation, and housing), who would each then be subject to re-election, after a specified period.[1] But such a development would reinforce narrow service perspectives and undermine the potential of local government as community governance.

Although there are benefits in enabling the public to judge performance of those responsible on a service-by-service basis, there are major disadvantages with this approach. It would not be a form of local government which facilitated an overall assessment of the needs and priorities of an area. It would not facilitate 'joined-up thinking' nor 'joined-up action'. The integration of services and functions in line with a wide-ranging vision for the future of an area would be almost impossible in these circumstances. There could be a requirement that these individuals form part of a 'Partnership', but without a mechanism for requiring commissioners to respond to the priorities of other commissioners, it would prove a relatively toothless innovation. And if the 'Partnership' were to be given significant powers, one would be back to a close approximation to an indirectly-elected local authority as currently exemplified by the Greater Manchester Combined Authority, which has recently been allocated a range of service responsibilities. It would reflect this model: a de facto local authority, but not directly-elected.

The requisite characteristics of a viable local government system

Wilson and Game identify a set of distinctive features of a viable local government system (2011, p37), as follows:

- a form of geographical and political decentralisation
- in which directly elected councils
- created by and subordinate to Parliament
- have partial autonomy
- to provide a wide variety of services, through various direct and indirect means
- funded in part by local taxation.

This list is a useful starting point in seeking to remedy the shortcomings of the current diminished role and status of local government. The various alternatives discussed earlier in this chapter – single-purpose authorities, indirectly elected authorities, and government-appointed bodies of local administration – would not be consistent with this widely recognised broad concept of what local government should entail. But in developing the case for a long-term solution, we would want to go beyond this set of 'minimum requirements'. It would, for example, be important to add an explicit clause referring to the role of local authorities in developing an overview of community needs and a responsibility to formulate a strategy to facilitate the well-being of the area, which includes the capacity for exercising significant local choice. This inclusion would highlight our emphasis on the importance of the community governance role. In addition, it is important that local choice should be exercised in a way which is responsive to the needs and priorities of local communities, to whom local authorities should be accountable through periodic elections, and that it should be facilitated by a scheme of local government finance which provides the budgetary flexibility to exercise local choice (a capacity very much limited by the current centrally imposed financial restrictions). All these themes are developed in Part II of this book; they are simply highlighted here to give a sense of our intentions. However, at this stage in the argument, it is helpful to discuss other potential strengths of local government, which should be recognised and exploited in the move to a strengthened, genuinely governmental system.

Core values of local government.

There are a further series of values which should form the building blocks of a healthy local government system. These values fit within Chandler's definition of the ethical (or moral) purposes of local government, which are to be distinguished from the efficiency-related purposes. They include (amongst others):

- building and articulating *community identity*;
- promoting citizenship and *participation*;
- dispersing power (*subsidiarity*).

These values are interrelated, and could usefully be synthesised into a wider principle of *localism* in a way that overcomes the confusion around the use of the term by the coalition government, following the 2010 election (see Chapter 3), and its subsequent ineffectiveness.

The importance of community identity

In recent years, the word 'community' has been used so loosely that it has become almost meaningless (the use of the term in the 2011 Localism Act provides one such example). But it has an interesting history and an emotive resonance, so it remains important to discuss it here. First, it needs to be distinguished from 'locality'. Whatever else it involves, the term 'community' implies some kind of network of social interaction, or nexus of social relationships. 'Locality', on the other hand, refers to a spatial territory which can be identified on a map, for example, an overspill estate or an inner-city neighbourhood. Neighbourhoods may contain within their boundaries significant levels of social interaction, to the extent that they can reasonably be characterised as 'communities' as Wilmott and Young discovered in Bethnal Green in the 1950s. But they do not necessarily possess this quality. It is unlikely that inner-city areas dominated by expensive blocks of flats aimed at upwardly mobile single people or childless couples would qualify in any meaningful sense as 'communities'. Second, it is important to acknowledge that, whilst 'community' has most commonly been linked with territorial space (that is, 'communities of place', such as mining villages, market towns, or seaside resorts), the term can also appropriately be applied to social groupings that are not location-specific, but are based on common interests or ethnic origins – for example, the gay community in Brighton or the Bangladeshi community in Tower Hamlets.

The extent to which locality-based communities still exist is an important consideration in assessing whether local government still matters to people as a manifestation of local identity and as an important mechanism for resolving local issues. It has been argued that the significance of 'community of place' has been eroded in recent times by increasing geographical mobility, which means that people now change their place of residence more frequently than they used to. As a result, the significance of their locality declines, as it comes increasingly to be seen as a temporary 'staging post' rather than a long-term commitment. However, the fact that there is now a wider range of choice of location available to a larger number of people could be argued to be enhancing, rather than undermining, the importance of place.

The typical stereotype used to illustrate this trend is the upwardly mobile young professional who is prepared to move to wherever the next promotion opportunity takes him or her (at least until a family is started, but often after that as well). In addition, such individuals are likely to be less dependent on the facilities of the neighbourhood in which they happen to live than most established residents. As car-owners, they will follow shopping opportunities and leisure pursuits wherever they are located, within a much wider ambit than the local neighbourhood.

While recognising the growth in geographical mobility ever since the end of World War II, it is important not to overemphasise its impact, particularly if the implication is drawn that the significance of 'community of place' has been greatly eroded. The basis of local democracy is where people live (and hence where they cast their votes), not where they work or carry out other activities.

In discussing the continuing significance of territory-based communities to the definition of local-government boundaries, the Banham Commission made an important distinction between 'effective' and 'affective' community. 'Effective community' refers to the patterns of activity (work, shopping, leisure activities) which can be identified in and around major centres of population and which were one of the driving forces behind the introduction of the Metropolitan County Councils in 1974. 'Affective community' refers to the sense of identity which people often feel with a particular spatial area: a town, a suburb, or a village. The concept is well illustrated by the loyalty and enthusiastic support generated by football teams at a range of spatial levels (from Manchester City to Derby County to Forest Green Rovers, a National League team from Nailsworth in the Cotswolds).

For affluent upwardly-mobile spiralists, the local neighbourhood may not have much significance in relation to activity patterns or local identity. However, for poorer families with limited (or no) access to a car, it remains of considerable significance. The journey to school or to the shops for a benefits-reliant single parent with several young children generates both a reliance on the local neighbourhood, and a concern that it should be a safe, clean, and (ideally) supportive place in which to live. Many local authorities have already introduced schemes which recognise the importance of local neighbourhoods, in some cases devolving limited budgets and decision-making powers to bodies on which both local councillors and local residents are represented.

One of the most important roles of local authorities is to respond to 'community' in both effective and affective terms, and as the Banham Commission discovered, there is ample evidence to confirm that local community identity at a range of different levels remains significant for large numbers of people. As we discuss in Chapter 8, it remains important that local authorities should, in principle, be defined in ways that match community, in both of these senses, a perspective which invariably strengthens the case for a multi-tier structure of local government.

The promotion of participation for an active democracy

Public participation can and does take place at all levels of government. In a sense, the act of voting (for MEP, MP, local councillor, or mayor) is an act of participation. But most critics of our system of democracy have argued that representative democracy (as characterised by voting opportunities) is a necessary but not a sufficient condition for a healthy democratic system, particularly at the local level. Participation opportunities at national (and European Economic Community (EEC) level) are limited to infrequent referenda (for example, over whether to remain in the EEC in 1975 and 2016), occasional mass demonstrations (for example, against the war in Iraq), the familiar lobbying practices of a wide range of interest and pressure groups, and the submission to the government of petitions. None of these mechanisms, however, offers much, if any, possibility of direct interaction between government and the governed.

At the local level, the opportunities for public participation, and the range of participatory mechanisms which are deployed are much greater (see Lowndes et al 2001), with considerable further potential for development. If there is a desire to encourage public participation, then this is the level where it can be most effective. Issues like the closure of schools, day centres, or libraries will often serve to stimulate participation, even if the authority has not sought it. Planning issues – housing redevelopments, inner-city ring roads, supermarkets, or 'bad neighbour' proposals – are likely to have similar repercussions. But participation can operate on a proactive as well as a reactive basis. Several authorities have instigated participation opportunities over budgetary options with an encouraging public response.

Local issues sometimes have to be taken seriously by MPs seeking election or re-election (note, for example, the success of the Independent parliamentary candidate Dr Richard Taylor in Kidderminster in 2001, accompanied by the successes in local elections of a Health Concern party, at least for a while, as a result of the downgrading of the local hospital). However, their impact upon the future of individual councillors and ruling parties or coalitions in local authorities is both more prevalent and potentially more threatening. Public participation should not necessarily be responded to positively, but it is important that it should be taken seriously by local authorities. On many local issues – for instance, those involving transportation and land-use planning   public opinion is often divided, and councils need to make judgements as to what weight to give to the different viewpoints involved. The strength of representative democracy lies in its capacity to promote a view of the public interest that transcends the special interests of managers, professionals, and other sectional interests.

Dispersing power

The third key value that underpins the case for a strong local government system is its role in the dispersal of power, which would not be possible under a system of unelected local administration. It is important that the power dispersed should be substantive, rather than symbolic. The power to make key decisions in a variety of fields (for example, local education and local planning matters) has been greatly eroded over the past 30 years. The ability to implement policies required by the centre that allow relatively little scope for local choice is a very limited form of discretionary power. Locality-affecting decisions made by those at the centre are typically made by those with little or no knowledge of local circumstances.

The Widdicombe Report puts it as follows:

> [T]he case for pluralism is that power should not be concentrated in one organisation of state, but should be dispersed, thereby providing political checks and balances and a restraint on arbitrary government and absolutism.
>
> *(Widdicombe 1986)*

The argument for the (maximum possible) dispersal of power is embodied in the principle of *subsidiarity*, which has been written into the European Charter of Local Self-Government. 'Subsidiarity', although far from the current reality of the distribution of central–local powers and responsibilities, has been widely accepted at least at a superficial level) by national parties and senior politicians within them. It is an important adjunct to the concept of localism, although this link was not made either by the last Labour government or the coalition which succeeded it. Subsidiarity has a range of important implications for the size and definition of local authorities, the number of councillors on them, the scope for 'neighbourhood working' within councils, and the possibilities of empowerment of (non-elected) local groups, within the framework of a representative system.

Although an emphasis on these three core values – community identity, public participation, and subsidiarity – is central to the reinvigoration of our beleaguered local government system, there are other ethical or moral considerations which should be incorporated. Local government has long provided valuable training for a political career at central government level. As Wilson and Game (2011, p51) point out, in the 2001 and 2005 Parliaments, more than half of all MPs had previously served as local councillors (two-thirds of Labour MPs, 60 per cent of Liberal Democrats, and 30 per cent of Conservatives). This pattern of movement from the locality to the centre is potentially beneficial in instilling an appreciation of local issues and governmental processes for those involved, much more so than in the case of the alternative 'professional political' career trajectory, in which individuals move from party researcher/adviser to MP, without the direct experience of responding to social, economic, and environmental challenges that becoming a local councillor necessarily provides (see Oborne 2001).

Local authorities are an important mechanism for fostering innovation and learning (a capacity highlighted and illustrated in Chapter 4). By responding to diverse local circumstances, and acting as the government of difference, local authorities can enhance the learning capacity of the governmental system as a whole, so long as it is open to such learning (Wilson and Game 2011, p46). And given that they are multi-service, multi-functional organisations, local authorities have a greater ability to respond 'swiftly, appropriately and corporately' to any local event or issue, more so than would a conglomeration of single-purpose agencies, elected or appointed. Effective coordination may not always be straightforward within one organisation, but it is infinitely more difficult amongst different organisations, which typically lack the incentive to subscribe to an overall vision for an area, or any multi-agency initiative that threatens their own assumptive worlds.

The need to reassess the role of local government

All of these ethical arguments for local government have been neglected in recent years. These arguments have not been overtly challenged or countered; rather, they have been conveniently pushed into the background, as individual government ministers have sought to impose their own priorities, when prior to 1979 there would have been much more consultation and exchange of views between the central and local government, before a way forward was agreed. Central government has the right to impose its priorities where national interests are involved, and where agreement cannot be reached, but it should be required to justify the case for doing so and it should be aware that the more it imposes its views, the more the governmental role of local authorities will be eroded.

As noted in the Introduction, this predisposition of the centre to impose is a relatively recent tendency in the historical pattern of central–local relations. In the decade preceding World War II, and again, once the post-war redistribution of responsibilities had been finalised (the transfer of the public utilities and health (except for public and environmental health) to the national level) there was a period of 30 years or so when the role and purpose of local government were mutually accepted by the two governmental levels, and, partly as a result, central–local relations were relatively unproblematic (compared with what came later) and, indeed, in many areas of activity, consensual (see Chapter 2). It was a time of expansion of public services, and the common practice (with some exceptions) was for central government to allocate any new function to local government, whilst seeking to influence the nature of the service by financial incentives (for example, high-rise flats) or advice (via circulars) and only in extremis by intervention, for which there was no general power. As Simon Jenkins points out that, before Kenneth Baker became secretary of state for education in 1987, there were only three legal requirements that local education authorities were required to meet. There was a similar degree of freedom in other local responsibilities, such as services for vulnerable children and elderly people, the provision of public housing, the production of structure plans and development control, and the provision of local transport infrastructure. There was no requirement to put services out to competitive tender, no attempt to regulate decision-making structures and processes, and no requirement that local authorities should work in partnership with the private sector or other public-sector agencies, although nothing to stop them doing so if they so wished. There was less need for formal partnerships at that time, because, apart from health and social security, the majority of local services were the direct responsibility of local government.[2] We are not arguing that the system worked perfectly, particularly in respect of its lack of responsiveness to public opinion (for example, over slum clearance and redevelopment processes – see Chapter 2). However, it was a relatively stable and harmonious era of central–local relationships. Aided by interconnected central–local professional networks, central government announced (in broad terms) what it wanted to happen and local government implemented it, in ways which central government generally found satisfactory.

That 'stable state' with its sense of consensus has been lost. It is right that it should have been challenged (as all 'stable states' should be). But in the process of continuing challenge, much of value has been lost. In particular, in an era notable for an emphasis on outsourcing, partnership working, excessive performance monitoring, and financial stringency, there is no longer a clear picture of what the role of local government in a unitary state should be, let alone a central–local consensus on this question. The problem is that the stable state has been progressively eroded, but in a disconnected way, with many of the central interventions owing more to the ambitions of individual ministers or ad hoc responses to perceived problems than to any semblance of a coherent vision on the part of the centre.

Having established the qualities that local government needs to re-establish itself as a democratically viable institution, responsive to local needs and empowered to deal with them, the following chapters explore in more detail how the current dysfunctional relationship between central and local government has developed, and what measures need to be taken to re-establish local government on a more appropriate and effective footing.

Notes

1 A system of this nature operates within many local government areas in the USA.
2 Although two-tier working outside the county boroughs was an important consideration.

2

HOW THE PAST CAN INFORM THE PRESENT

Five stages in the development of local government

Introduction

There is a widespread acceptance that the period since the election of the Conservative/Liberal Democrat coalition proved an extremely difficult time for local government, with little prospect or evidence of improvement following the election of a Conservative government in May 2015. 'Damage limitation' is the term that best characterises this period in local government's history. Indeed, when we consider – as we do below – the different stages in the development of local government since the mid-19th century, a strong case can be made that the current stage is the bleakest in its history, a period when its status and influence in the governmental arrangements of Britain was at a nadir.

How can this gloomy conclusion be justified? There are two linked strands to the argument. First, there have been the draconian cuts in expenditure (and services) that local authorities have been required to make (which go well beyond anything experienced in the Thatcher era), a process whose negative impact upon local services intensified over the five-year period of the coalition government, with an apparently unconcerned Eric Pickles, the secretary of state for communities and local government, enthusiastically volunteering such cuts, rather than seeking (as is the usual practice for ministers) to defend the activity for which he is responsible. While local authorities have fulfilled their part of this (imposed) bargain, the severity of the cuts have necessarily involved the depletion of a range of discretionary services, which have long been valued (and in many cases taken for granted) by local people. Few, if any, local authorities have relished the process, but they have recognised that it has had to be done, and they have done it. The argument is not that the Coalition Government was wholly responsible for local government's unenviable situation. The likelihood is that, in the circumstances, any government would have felt it necessary to require significant cuts in local expenditure. However, the process could certainly have been handled more sympathetically and supportively than it was.

Second, the requirement to make severe cuts in expenditure meant that there was little scope for the more wide-ranging governmental role of local authorities: developing innovative solutions to local problems that transcend their statutory requirements to provide a range of specific personal and environmental services, like education and highways, and to regulate areas of local activity, such as land-use and licensed premises. It becomes increasingly difficult, during a resource famine, for a local authority to justify expenditure on non-essential projects, like a new Arts Centre, when to do so would involve a further cut in those services that the council was required to provide. There have been pots of money, including specific grants and Lottery funding, available for selected activities of this nature. But it has been much more difficult to finance them than at any time since the end of World War II, or indeed since well before that. The inclusion of a general power of competence in the 2012 Local Government Act has been of little help in such circumstances, although it may be in the future.

Currently, local government's community governance role is greatly diminished. There is continuing evidence of some authorities developing imaginative responses to dealing with the unprecedented financial challenges facing them – for example, Lambeth's adoption of a 'John Lewis' approach to service provision. But the last five to six years of both Coalition and Conservative government has certainly *not* been a 'golden age' for local government.

Has there ever been a golden age? How would we recognise it, and what characteristics were displayed in it that would need to be built into an agenda to rehabilitate the institution of local government in the future? In considering this question, it is necessary to reflect on the history of local government, as a means to helping us understand how we have reached the current position and what needs to be done to change it. Our review is not comprehensive. It starts in about 1870, and covers some decades in more detail than others. We have identified four pre-2010 eras, which we have characterised as 'Municipal Enterprise', 'Municipal Socialism', 'The Era of Services Domination', and 'The Increasing Domination of the Centre'.

Stage 1: Municipal Enterprise (1870–1914)

A constant reference point in historical reviews of local government is what was achieved in the City of Birmingham, under the leadership of Joseph Chamberlain, from the 1870s onwards. Under Chamberlain's leadership, the city council dealt proactively with a range of problems in an attempt to improve the quality of life in the city. It was not then characterised as community governance, but that is what, in effect, it was. The provision of statutory services played a more limited role than it later did in Birmingham (and elsewhere), particularly after World War II. Public utilities – gas, electricity, and water – were provided by undertakings established by the city council (and later by large numbers of other local councils), not to all households, but to a significant proportion of them. The worst slum areas were cleared and their inhabitants rehoused in council-provided accommodation. Public transport in the form of trams and (later) buses was introduced. Libraries were established. Many of the schemes were introduced through the promotion of private bills in Parliament. It was an impressive example of municipal enterprise.

Not only Birmingham embarked on major improvement schemes of this nature. Other large cities – Manchester, Sheffield, Liverpool, and, in particular, Glasgow – followed suit. Progress in London was slower, mainly because of the complex patchwork of local government arrangements there, centred on the Metropolitan Board of Works (the London County Council was not established until 1888, and the London boroughs until 1899). The more rural areas lacked the resources and motivation to drive forward such improvements (county councils and lower-tier authorities within them were not established until 1888 and 1894, respectively). Even after the county councils were created, they were typically dominated by parties (Conservative, Progressives, Ratepayers) which were more cautious in their approach to public expenditure than Chamberlain had been. Municipal enterprise was largely an initiative driven by the larger provincial cities.

The spread of this kind of approach was impressive and, where it was taken forward enthusiastically in several ways, justified the epithet of a 'golden age' (albeit one that was city focused). In his introduction to *Half a Century of Municipal Decline 1935–1985* (Loughlin et al 1985), John

Griffith quotes from the *Everyman Encyclopaedia* of 1913, which said this about local government:

> Perhaps the most remarkable feature of modern local government is the rapid advance of municipal trading ... (a policy) which is so antithetical to the doctrine of laissez faire and such a complete subversion of the time-worn notion that state functions end with the conservation of internal order and the defence of aggression from without, that many stigmatise it with the name of municipal socialism ... the increase within the last thirty years is unquestionably due partly to the progress in municipal trading enterprise ... experience shows that municipalities are not embarrassed by the added duties involved in providing and managing tramways, railways, omnibuses, steamboats and fire insurance, the supply of electrical fittings, clothing, confectionery, in school, milk and eggs and in brick-making and tailoring ... the whole question is one of opinion whether or not the interests of civilisation are better served by the state becoming its own shopkeeper and factory owner, instead of allowing the private individual to exploit other individuals or companies for gain.

In this sense, 'municipal enterprise' can be regarded as a major force within the political climate of the time, challenging the traditional laissez-faire liberalism of the 19th century, which proved an inspiration for the later development of 'municipal socialism' (see below). We wish to emphasise here the proactive, innovative governmental character of the municipal-enterprise era. That capacity for community governance has waxed and waned since, and is currently dormant, but remains a key requisite of a healthy local government system.

Stage 2: Municipal Socialism (1919–1939)

If Birmingham is the best-documented example of municipal enterprise, Bermondsey is its equivalent for municipal socialism. As with municipal enterprise its roots lay in a genuine concern for the well-being of the local population, which transcended any requirements to provide a range of statutory services. Chamberlain's equivalent in Bermondsey was Dr Alfred Salter, the Labour leader of Bermondsey Borough Council in the 1920s and 1930s (Labour first won a majority on the council in 1922). There were other hotbeds of municipal socialism: Stepney (where Clement Attlee was mayor in the early 1920s), Hackney (where Herbert Morrison was mayor and leader), and Poplar (George Lansbury, likewise). In all of these authorities, there was a propensity to challenge what were seen as inappropriate policies of central government. But the key element of municipal socialism in Bermondsey (and in other like-minded councils) was its determination to do all it could to improve the health, living conditions, and aspirations of its largely working-class population.

Amongst the initiatives introduced in Bermondsey in the Salter era was a 'greening of the borough', which involved the planting of trees in nearly every street, a proliferation of flower beds and window boxes, and the development of open spaces for recreational use. The process was supervised by the aptly named Beautification Committee. Second, there was an ambitious scheme – partially realised – to demolish two-thirds of the borough's substandard housing, and replace it with 'garden city'-type developments. Third, in response to the prevalence of tuberculosis, several imaginative measures were introduced, including the provision of open-air shelters for patients returning from a sanatorium, the encouragement of tubercular-tested milk, the reservation of beds in a Swiss sanatorium for Bermondsey residents, and eventually the building of a sanatorium within Bermondsey itself. Fourth, there was the construction of a state-of-the-art public baths with a range of facilities that went well beyond normal provision in similar areas, and a free library (see Brockway 1949, pp85–114 for further details).

Some features of the 'Bermondsey revolution' distinguished it from its Birmingham equivalent, 50 years previously. The first was the strength of the link between the council and the local community. As Sue Goss (1988) shows in her historical study of the politics of Southwark (into which Bermondsey was incorporated in 1965), the council's radical programme of change was developed and implemented with the widespread support and indeed involvement of local people. Labour party membership was high and active. Public participation was a reality in 1930s Bermondsey in a way it rarely is today.

Second, the Bermondsey revolution was implemented, at least in its later stages, in the kind of difficult economic circumstances that have parallels with the current recession. From 1922 to 1929, the rates were reduced by 20 per cent despite the ambitious development programme (because of the 'efficient and business-like' management of the council, according to Brockway). In the 1930s during the time of the Great Depression, rates were considerably higher, and the council faced rebukes from the government about the level of its expenditure and rates (Goss 1988). However, rate-capping had not then been dreamt of, and there was nothing to stop the council financing whatever level of expenditure it wished from the rates, subject to local people being prepared to respond positively at the next local election, which, in Bermondsey, proved to be the case. The link between local expenditure and local accountability was more transparent then than it is now.

Municipal socialism had a major impact in Bermondsey during the 1920s and 1930s. It improved the quality of life of a relatively poor community in a range of imaginative ways. It provided a further example of community governance in action. The starting point for the programme of action was Alfred Salter's perception of the problems of the borough, not merely a review of priorities between service responsibilities. His vision and plan of action had strong roots of support in the local community. However, although it can be argued that it was a golden age of local government in Bermondsey, this was not a nation-wide phenomenon. As Goss (1988) shows, even the two other adjacent Labour-controlled London boroughs (Camberwell and Southwark) proved much less innovative and visionary. It was mainly a Labour-specific phenomenon, although by no means all Labour-controlled councils adopted it. In so far as one can judge, it was the dominant ethos in only a handful of London boroughs, the London County Council (under Herbert Morrison), and a few provincial outposts. Among the provincial City bosses of the 1930s, by no means all shared Salter's visionary approach, nor his emphasis on the importance of public involvement. And the shire counties were still largely Conservative or Independent dominated, and correspondingly less inclined towards radical action of any kind.

Stage 3: The Era of Services Domination (1945–1979)

In what sense, if any, did the 30 years following World War II represent a 'golden age' for British local government? The era did not start promisingly. The newly-elected Labour government soon demonstrated centralist tendencies, epitomised by the transfer of the majority of health functions (including hospitals) from the purview of local authorities to the newly established National Health Service (NHS), although public and environmental health remained with councils, and the nationalisation of the public utilities – gas, electricity, and water – although the fire service was returned to local government control. Compared with its heyday in the early 1930s, local government appeared to have been seriously weakened by 1948.

However, these losses of functions were counter-balanced by the acquisition of a new range of service responsibilities over the next decade and, in many cases, increased activity and responsibility in established service domains between 1948 and 1979. Throughout this period there was continuous growth in local government activity and expenditure, partly inspired by the challenge of dealing with the devastation and disruption caused by the war. Town planning emerged as a high-profile local activity, both forward planning – setting out schemes for the allocation of land use and introduction of transportation links in the urban areas – and development control. In both cases, local authorities operated with a degree of autonomy that has declined progressively since the 1980s. The planning and construction of estates of council-built housing grew cumulatively from the early 1950s onwards, only falling back in the 1970s. The implementation of the 1944 Education Act, introducing a tripartite system of secondary education, was left largely to local authorities, with a significant degree of flexibility in how they interpreted the act, although the government could and did use capital expenditure controls to influence education policy, particularly in the drive to comprehensive education. Local authorities had considerable discretion over the school curriculum, to an extent that seems scarcely credible in the current political climate. Personal social services grew steadily over the period, encompassing children, the elderly, the mentally ill (outside hospital), the mentally handicapped, and the physically disabled, which were consolidated in 1974 by the creation of generic social services departments. In the cities, large numbers of slum properties after inspection by public health inspectors were designated as unfit, and demolished before the redevelopment of the area concerned. Ring roads were designed and built, traffic and pedestrians separated, and leisure centres constructed. It was a time of frenetic public-sector activity, much of it encouraged (or indeed required) by central government, but without the level of central control over the detail of the services provided that is apparent today.

The key instrument of government influence was the circular, which consisted of 'advice' rather than 'requirement'. Circulars were taken extremely seriously within most local authorities, more so perhaps than they need to have been. Capital expenditure controls were used by central government when it wished to be more directive. It is an indication of the transformation of the central–local climate that circulars have since more or less disappeared from view, replaced by more binding legislative or quasi-legislative regulations.

The financial mechanism of the rates continued to give local authorities a degree of financial flexibility that has diminished substantially since then.

The ability of authorities to impose rates on local businesses, as well as on local householders, enhanced this flexibility.

Several aspects of the way in which local government operated from 1945 to 1975 would suggest that this period might merit the epithet of a 'golden age'. There was a continuous growth in local government expenditure and a lack of interference by central government as to how it should be spent. Local authorities played a key role in transforming towns and cities after the war, with the 'new profession' of town planning playing a leading part in the process. Education and social services both grew in importance, and, in both cases, local authorities operated with a high level of autonomy.

There are, however, reasons to be circumspect about viewing the 1945–1979 period as a golden age. The activities of local authorities were focused on particular priorities: urban renewal, dealing with the pressure of increased car ownership, and the three big service-blocks of education, social services, and (council) housing. Inter-departmental cooperation was required for urban renewal and transportation planning, although it was often bedevilled by inter-professional rivalries between – for example, highways surveyors and town planners, and housing officers and architects. This age was one of departmental autonomy, typified by the characterisation of the local education service as 'the education authority', as though it were somehow separate from the council as a corporate entity, which in practice it often effectively was. With some exceptions, major innovations took place within service areas, not between them, and were in most cases dominated by the current 'good-practice' ethos of the professions concerned, which in several cases have by no means stood the test of time. It was the era of urban motorways and ring roads (traffic engineers), high-rise flats (housing architects), slum clearance (later reduced in scope as housing improvement became a favoured alternative), green belts, and institutional social care (later overtaken by community care).

The professional networks spanned both central and local government. In constructing high-rise flats and ring roads, and focusing on slum clearance schemes, local authorities were acting with the encouragement and support of their central government counterparts. There was little tension between the two levels of government. The professions knew best, or thought they did, and local councils (councillors and officers alike) invariably went along with professional advice. There were exceptions; some towns decided that high-rise flats were not for them. Tameside refused to relinquish its grammar schools, at a time when almost all authorities were embracing the comprehensive ideal. However, the sense of a professionally underpinned central/local consensus about what needed to be done prevailed. There were local innovations: Cambridgeshire and Leicestershire continued to develop the 'Community College' idea, involving schools in a much richer set of links with the local community than was the norm.

The dominance of the professions was not at the time balanced by a strong managerial leadership role, later personified by the 'chief executive'. Chief executives only began to emerge in the later years of the era. Until then 'town clerks' and 'county clerks' still dominated, their background and perspective mostly a legalistic one.

In the mid-1970s, the ideas of corporate management and corporate planning began to emerge (heavily influenced by the Maud and Bains reports, and by Professor John Stewart at the Institute of Local Government Studies at Birmingham University). Both were conceived as an antidote to departmentalism and over-reliance on professional opinion. Both can be linked with the perceived need for local authorities to act as organs of community governance, in addition to their familiar role as service providers. The ideas of corporate planning and management (and indeed community governance) increased in influence in the late 1970s, and more so in the 1980s, when the central–local political context was very different; but from 1945 to 1975 they were still at an embryonic stage. It is the dominance of the 'service provision' ethos during the 1945–1979 period that dilutes the case for it being seen as a 'golden age' of local government.

A further cause of disappointment about this era resulted from the government's response to the Report of the Layfield Committee on Local Government Finance in 1977. The Layfield Report, having identified confusion as to where accountability for the level of local-government expenditure lay, argued convincingly that a choice had to be made between a financial system based on central accountability and one based on local accountability. This choice would itself reflect a more fundamental choice as to whether local authorities should primarily be seen as agents of central government or as (largely) autonomous decision-making governmental agencies in their own right. The Labour government missed the opportunity to make either of these choices, and to clarify local government's constitutional position, preferring instead a woolly 'middle-way' emphasising 'partnership': 'The Government sees the duties and responsibilities involved in the provision of local services as being shared on a partnership basis between central and local government' (HMSO Cmnd 6813 1977, pp4–5).

Later in the century an enthusiasm for 'partnership working' was instrumental in blurring local accountability, and the capacity for accountable local choice. And local government finance has continued to suffer from the failure to confront the choice posed by Layfield.

Stage 4: The increasing dominance of the centre (1979–2010)

By 1976 it had become clear that the inexorable central government-fuelled rise in local expenditure had to be halted, hence the famous 'the party's over' speech by Anthony Crosland in 1976. The era of ever-increasing local spending on services (and urban renewal) was drawing to a close. But what was to replace it?

Had Labour won the 1979 election, a different era might have developed. But a Conservative victory, under a leader with an antipathy towards local government, accentuated by the rapid progress made by the Labour left in local authorities in London and several of the big provincial cities in the early 1980s, set the scene for a period in which the powers of local government were cumulatively diminished, and the role of the centre correspondingly enhanced.

This era, or at least the Conservative-dominated part of it, has been powerfully and perceptively chronicled by Simon Jenkins in *Accountable to None* (Jenkins 1994). In chapter after chapter he describes and explains the increasing central dominance of a whole range of services and aspects of local government: finance (rate-capping, and the introduction of the poll tax); housing (council-house sales and the ban on council-house construction); education (the national curriculum, the 'grant-maintained status' schools initiative); higher education (polytechnics were removed from local authority control in 1988); local planning responsibilities (the introduction of urban development corporation, or UDCs, and enterprise zones); and the requirement to put selective services out to tender (compulsory competitive tendering, or CCT, introduced in 1987 and extended in 1990). Local council involvement in running the police service was diluted (Police and Magistrates Courts Act 1994). Authorities that had proved a political nuisance to the prime minister (the Greater London Council, or GLC, and the six metropolitan county councils) were abolished and their responsibilities distributed amongst a plethora of borough councils, joint boards, and joint committees (the last two involving a blurring of accountability).

The various measures discussed by Jenkins all involved the dilution or increased regulation of local service provision (for example, education and CCT), the total withdrawal of local service responsibilities (polytechnics), decreased local financial autonomy and flexibility (rate-capping), use of central initiatives to replace local responsibilities in specified areas (UDCs), and arbitrary politically inspired reorganisations (GLC, local education authority (LEA)). In no sense could this period be construed as a golden age of British local government.

The perception that the 1979–1997 period was a profoundly discouraging time for local government is widely (and justifiably) acknowledged. But it has been argued there were two redeeming features. Atkinson and Wilks-Heeg (2000, p15), in their thought-provoking book *Local Government from Thatcher to Blair*, question the dominant view that the period was one of unmitigated 'bad news':

> We did begin to ask whether local government was actually in need of saving … despite the onslaught (1979–97) it was evident to us that local government not only remained a sizeable part of the British state, it also continued to be the source of important policy innovation … its redefinition had not come entirely from the centre – a good deal of fresh thinking had been done by the local government community itself … there were a whole host of ways in which local authorities in the UK had sought to defend their independent policy-making role.

If Atkinson and Wilks-Heeg are right, then a picture emerges of at least some local authorities exploiting their (diminishing) level of autonomy from central government to resist central pressure, and devise new ways of responding to local problems, a key feature of the idea of 'community governance'. They use the concept of 'creative autonomy' to characterise the process they are describing and argue that it was manifested in the way that authorities dealt with rate-capping (for example, the 'creative accounting' techniques adopted in Ken Livingstone's GLC and in other left-wing Labour councils), their preparedness to work constructively with the private and voluntary sectors (not necessarily in ways advocated by central government), the way they took seriously Agenda 21 (which encouraged local authorities to develop environmental sustainability plans for their areas), and their preparedness to explore and exploit new resources that stemmed from our membership of the EEC. Most important was the emergence of the economic development function, which provides an example of a local initiative to deal with a local problem, leading to the government giving local authorities an explicit power to do so (thereby increasing the potential for central control). It is an impressive list, and although Atkinson and Wilks-Heeg perhaps overstate their case, their arguments provide a viable counterbalance to the sense that 'it was all doom and gloom'.

The second redeeming feature of the period was the increasing propensity of local authorities to develop corporate strategies, which, at their best, incorporated a distinctive locally-influenced view both of priorities and of what kind of authority the council was striving to become. Many corporate strategies were vacuous documents, dominated by high-level platitudinous objectives with which no one would be likely to disagree: 'good quality housing for all at prices all can afford'. But an influential Local Government Management Board publication *Fitness for Purpose* (Leach and Lowndes 1994) demonstrated that responses to the government's agenda for local government varied considerably, illustrating that big choices were still available to local authorities and were being made, although many authorities were more inclined to 'muddle through'.

Fitness for Purpose identified four different broad strategies within the world of local government. First, there was 'traditionalism' that involved 'fighting to stay the same'. A good example of this approach is the way in which several (typically old-school Labour) authorities sought to 'manage' the CCT process, so that as many contracts as possible were won by in-house direct labour organisations. However questionable this manoeuvring, it illustrates a determination to resist unpopular central government pressure, in a way that demonstrates a time-honoured local-government practice of finding scope for 'interpretation' within legislation that can be used to limit its (perceived) undesirable effects.

Other authorities enthusiastically embraced the commercial ideology underpinning the government's vision ('Brent plc'; 'Braintree means business'), while yet others (particularly the cities and larger towns) sought to transform themselves, using the range of economic development and external funding opportunities discussed by Atkinson and Wilks-Heeg (for example, Birmingham's attempt to upgrade its status to that of an 'international' city). Finally, some authorities such as Tower Hamlets decentralised council services to such an extent that the central core of the authority was untypically small. Most of the activities of the borough came to be focused on the 'real communities': Poplar, Bethnal Green, Stepney, and Bow.

It can be argued that although the 1979–1997 period involved a major shift to centralisation, involving a formidable array of restrictions on and removal of responsibilities from local authorities, there remained the capacity for substantive local choice, illustrated by the distinctive strategic approaches noted above.

Three other features of this era are significant. First there was the process of juridification, well documented by Loughlin (1996). This term refers to the government's increasing tendency to rely on legislative measures including statutory instruments, rather than informal channels to seek to ensure that the changes it sought to introduce in the operations of local authorities were implemented. Juridification led in turn to an increasing tendency for local authorities to challenge aspects of the government's legislative programme in the courts. The volume of local-government legislation during this period was unprecedented, as were the number of legal challenges in response to it. The more consensual government circular had by then entirely disappeared as a tool of central influence.

Second, during this period, the government saw fit for the first time to involve itself in the internal workings of local authorities, both over political issues (Widdicombe Committee of Inquiry into the Conduct of Local Government Business, 1986, and the Act of Parliament that followed it, 1989) and over managerial issues, with the requirement for local authorities to appoint 'monitoring officers' and 'heads of paid service', as well as the impact of the CCT legislation. This readiness set a precedent, which, as we shall see, the succeeding Labour government was only too ready to follow.

Third, there was a new emphasis on 'customer care', linked to a wider concern with service improvement. Previously it had been unusual to hear users of local-government services referred to as 'consumers' or 'customers'.

Then came the 1997 general election and the return of a Labour government, which retained office until 2010. Great was the rejoicing in the town and county halls across the country, and not just in Labour- and Liberal Democrat-controlled authorities. The (relatively few) remaining Conservative-controlled authorities had not welcomed their party's dismissive attitude to local government. There was a widespread expectation that the new Labour government would restore the status of local government in the (unwritten) constitution by reallocating powers that had been transferred to central government or to QUANGOS, and by freeing up choice within the service areas for which local government had retained responsibility.

It was a false dawn. Although many encouraging noises were made (Tony Blair even wrote – or gave his name to – a pamphlet entitled *Leading the Way: A New Vision for Local Government* (1998)), the expected reversal of the process of centralisation, which gathered momentum during the 1979–1997 period, did not take place. Indeed, it accelerated. As Simon Jenkins points out (Jenkins 2006) both Tony Blair and Gordon Brown turned out to be inveterate centralisers, uneasy about allowing local opportunities to do anything that might challenge or undermine Labour's 'public services' vision (or rebound on them in a way that might adversely affect re-election prospects). Most of the first batch of local-government legislation was focused on internal structures and processes, the provisions for elected mayors and local cabinets, the abolition of the committee system and the introduction of scrutiny mechanisms, the replacement of CCT with the 'Best Value' regime, and the setting up of 'local strategic partnerships' and 'community strategies'. Whatever the merits of these innovations, none restored lost service responsibilities or created new ones. There was no resurrection of the power to build council housing, no reduction in the central domination of the education service, and no change to the local-government financial regime, where the continued dominance of central grant severely restricted the flexibility to increase local council expenditure, because of the 'unbalanced' 'gearing effect' of increases in Council Tax (a 1 per cent increase in council expenditure typically required a 4 per cent increase in council tax). The scope for choice in planning was further reduced rather than widened, particularly in the mid-2000s.

The 2001 election was followed by a further raft of inspectorial and regulatory measures that went beyond anything devised by the preceding Conservative government. The introduction of the Comprehensive Performance Assessment (CPA) system from 2002 onwards, which was managed by the ever-growing Audit Commission, differed from previous inspectorial measures in that it sought to provide an overall measure of the performance of all local authorities, and to penalise those authorities who were deemed to have performed badly. The seeds of managerial (and political) interference and regulation, sown in the later years of the Conservative governments, were nurtured and sustained, rather than uprooted.

There followed in 2006 yet another example of what governments do when they run out of ideas, namely the initiation of an unnecessary and appallingly-implemented structural reorganisation (see Chisholm and Leach 2008).

Six key themes can be extracted when reviewing Labour's overall programme for local government between 1997 and 2010 (see Leach 2010): the move to executive government, an emphasis on 'strong leadership', a further development of partnership working, the strengthening of the performance/inspection culture, a concern with community engagement and community cohesion, and a further move towards unitary authorities. All of these measures involve changes to structures, processes, or regulatory procedures. None involved a strengthening of local authorities' responsibilities or capacity to make meaningful local choices. In retrospect, 1997–2010 was a hugely disappointing period for local government, although patches of innovation continued, despite the lack of incentive provided by the centre. It justifies its link with the previous 17 years of Conservative rule as an era characterised as 'the drift to centralism', a conclusion that was not anticipated in 1997.

Stage 5: Damage Limitation (2010–2015)

We have already outlined the justification for the argument that local government is currently experiencing what is perhaps its bleakest time within the whole period discussed in this chapter (1875 to the present day). Despite some fine rhetoric in the Conservative's party's pre-election policy paper (*Control Shift: Returning Power to Local Communities*), nothing that they and their coalition partners have done justified the intentions expressed in this title. There has been much talk of localism, but a lack of clarity about what it was supposed to mean (see Chapter 3). It did not appear to mean the empowerment of local authorities. Very few of the centralising measures introduced by the Labour government were reversed, apart from a retreat from regionalisation, and a dilution of the performance targets regime associated with the Audit Commission. Local councils have been required to make drastic cuts in expenditure as part of the government's contested strategy of cutting public expenditure to stimulate economic growth. Communities and Local Government Secretary Eric Pickles adopted an aggressive rather than supportive tone from the start (despite his own experience as council leader of Bradford in the early 1990s). The one positive change has been the transfer of the public health service from the NHS back into local government (from whence it had been removed in 1974). The potential synergy of linking a responsibility for public health with the responsibility for education, housing, and range of other local authority services is considerable.

The record of the coalition over local government is discussed further in Chapter 3. It represents the antithesis of a 'golden age'.

Conclusion: Has there ever been a golden age?

If pressed, we would endorse the view of Wilson and Game (2011, p59) that 'the closest approximation to a golden age of local government was probably the early 1930s'.

During these years, a system of multi-functional, elected, and genuinely local authorities were the providers of more major services to its citizens than at any time before or since. Raising much more of their revenue from their own local rates than from central government grants, these authorities were substantially free from detailed central direction and intervention. A thriving local government was even valued as part of the democratic defence against fascism. The period was a high-water mark.

During this time local authorities briefly acquired the responsibility for income support, and unemployment assistance, taking over the role of the poor law system with its infamous workhouses from 1929 until 1934. Bearing in mind the breadth of the council's vision in places like Alfred Salter's Bermondsey, and the readiness to respond to the full range of 'social, economic and environmental needs of local people' (to quote the wording of the Local Government Act 1980), it can be seen that community governance flourished at this time, although in some authorities more than others, coupled with the existence of wide-ranging service-provision powers, typically involving much greater scope for local discretion and choice than exists in the present day.

The quote from Wilson and Game gives clues to many of the features of a healthy local government system that have since been lost, and need to be restored, if local government is to regain its former status and fulfil its potential. Is local government still 'multifunctional'? Yes, but significantly less so. Are authorities 'genuinely local'? In many cases, no. Kirklees, Tameside, Cheshire East, and Sefton are all artificial constructs, invoking little sense of community identity, and there are many other such examples (see Chapter 8). Do local authorities raise most of their resources from local revenue sources? Quite the contrary. Are they substantially free of detailed central direction and intervention? They are not. There is a long road of rehabilitation to travel.

3

THE MYTH OF LOCALISM

Introduction

The previous chapter noted that the five years of the coalition government (2010–2015) had been a dispiriting time for local government. But in the immediate aftermath of the 2010 general election it was not apparent that it would continue to be so. Although the need for significant reductions in public expenditure (including local government) had been made clear from the start, this policy was counterbalanced by one that implied a more positive future for local government, namely a commitment to 'localism'. This (admittedly imprecise) concept had been flagged up in the Conservative party's 2009 green paper (*Control Shift; Returning Power to Local Communities*), in which there were indications that the Conservative party was intending to reverse the cumulative centralising tendencies of its 1979–1997 period in office, and of the Labour governments that followed. It included the following passage:

> By giving power and financial incentives to local authorities to foster growth, we can start to move towards a national economy that is built from strong, vibrant, local economies – an economy that is far less vulnerable to global shocks or the failures of a few dominant industries.
>
> *(Conservative Party 2009, p1)*

While this statement was concerned specifically with economic development, the document expressed similar intentions in other spheres of local

activity, and David Cameron himself made clear his localist credentials
(Conservative Party 2009, p1):

> I am a strong localist, for one simple reason. I know that the small, the
> personal and the local work with the grain of human nature and not
> against it. But this is not some romantic attachment to the patterns of
> our past. Localism holds the key to economic, social and political success
> in the future.

The coalition government's post-election programme confirmed these
sentiments:

> The Government believes that it is time for a fundamental shift of
> power from Westminster to people. We will promote decentralisation
> and democratic engagement, and we will end the era of top-down
> government by giving new powers to local councils, communities,
> neighbourhoods and individuals ... the government will promote the
> radical devolution of power and greater financial autonomy to local
> government and community groups.
>
> *(TSO 2010, p11)*

This undifferentiated amalgam of 'councils, neighbourhoods, communities
and individuals' reflected a basic ambiguity in the coalition government's
policies. Clarification was needed here as to what precisely was to be
devolved to each of these entities. But, on the face of it, these pronouncements
sounded like good news for local authorities, and were congruent with a
longstanding Conservative tradition (abandoned, possibly temporarily, in
the 1979–1997 period) of limited central interference in the operation of
local government.

There was some encouragement, too, in the appointment of Eric Pickles
as the secretary of state for communities and local government. He had
been leader of Bradford City Council 20 years previously, when he was
seen as a Thatcherite apostle. But at least he had an inside knowledge of
how local authorities worked, and, it was hoped, could be relied upon to
reflect this understanding in his dealings with them.

The new government's commitment to localism was quickly channelled
into the Localism Bill, which Greg Clark, minister of state in the Department for Communities and Local Government (DCLG), referred to in the
following terms:

For the best part of a century, most Acts that have passed through this House have taken power from communities and councils and given more power to Central Government or in some cases to European government. This is an historic [*sic*] Act, not just for the measures it contains but for what it represents. It is about striking out in a different direction. Power should be held at the lowest possible level. We want this to be the first Parliament for many years that, by the end of its Sessions, will have given power away.

(House of Commons, Statement 7 November 2011)

At the same time, however, there were some contradictory messages stemming from the secretary of state. In the first post-election *Comprehensive Spending Review*, Eric Pickles appeared keen to demonstrate his political stature in the new government by cutting local government's spending disproportionately (compared with other central departments), seeking perhaps to gain political kudos by 'settling first' with the chancellor. He also embarked on an attack on chief executives' salaries, which are in fact modest in comparison with those enjoyed by managers of equivalent status in the private sector and in other public-sector bodies. His attempt to secure the reintroduction of weekly refuse collections – surely a matter for local choice – was another worrying development.

The prime minister's 'big idea' of the 'big society' was launched before the 2010 election (see Seldon and Snowden 2016, pp147–164), without the links between it and the localism agenda being made clear. One interpretation of this concept was that it was (inter alia) an attempt to motivate local community groups to volunteer to take over responsibility for local services, which councils might increasingly struggle to maintain (for example, libraries, arts centres, and recreational and community facilities.). Seldon and Snowden argue that the prime minister, inspired by Steve Hilton, was genuinely committed to the idea, but it failed to sustain its momentum in the face of indifference from other government departments, and the more pressing nature of other issues (the economy, Europe, the London riots of 2011). It had virtually disappeared from the policy agenda by early 2012.

Despite the worthy sentiments expressed by Greg Clark and others, the Localism Act (2011) proved a disappointment for four main reasons. First, although the act contained one or two measures that 'freed up' local authorities, it contained several that had the opposite effect. Second, there was a 'fatal ambiguity' in the act about the 'balance of empowerment' between local councils and local communities. Third, the key issue of local-government finance was virtually ignored. Finally, there was little or no evidence that the commitment to localism, which the Localism Act purported to embody, was shared by other departments of state that had responsibility for services delivered by local authorities (for example, Department for Education, Home Office, and Department of Health). Indeed, some of the services within the purview of the DCLG itself were taken forward in ways that appeared at odds with the government's localist commitment.

A Localism Act or a Centralism Act

To what extent did the Localism Act involve a dilution of centralism and a related strengthening of the role of local authorities? Regional strategies were to be abolished, as were the Comprehensive Area Assessments; ring-fenced central grants to local authorities were to be phased out; a range of planning regulations were withdrawn; and more choice was provided in political decision-making arrangements, including a return to the committee system. But on the face of it, the most striking localist commitment was the introduction of 'a general power of competence' for local government.

On the debit side, the act included more than 100 new powers and regulations, including provisions to change planning processes in a way that would (further) centralise planning outcomes; restrictions on local-authority newspapers; a requirement for referenda on the introduction of elected mayors to be held in the 12 largest city councils; and, most worryingly, a council-tax freeze.

The terms in which the 'general power of competence' were expressed in the act were strange. Previously, this provision had been characterised as a 'power of general competence' that facilitated local authorities doing whatever they wished for their citizens and areas, as long as that power had not been expressly forbidden, or given to another body. The Localism Act gave councils 'the power to do anything individuals generally may do', which appeared to introduce an element of confusion about the scope of the power, and raised the question of how it differed from the existing power councils have to do 'anything which contributes to the social, economic or environmental well-being of its area'. Also of concern was the fact that the judicial doctrine of 'ultra vires' was not sufficiently reduced in scope.

Furthermore, there was a sting in the tail of the provision of this power. Power was given to the secretary of state to 'make orders to prevent local authorities from doing anything specified in the orders', which, as Jones and Stewart (2011, p14) point out, undermines the whole point of the general power of competence. Eric Pickles told the Commons at the Bill's second reading that 'he needed to retain residual powers, just in case'. The implication is that central government needed the power to overrule a local authority 'just in case' it wanted to do something the government disliked, which if widely used would have worrying implications for the reduction of the scope of local choice.

The act introduced several new powers and rights for local communities, including the following:

- The 'Community Right to Challenge' gave local community groups, parish councils, and council employees the right to express an interest in running a local-authority service. If the challenge were to be accepted the challenging organisation was then able to bid as part of a procurement exercise to take over a particular service.
- The 'Community Right to Bid' gave community groups a chance to bid for assets listed as having a community value. Community groups that expressed an interest would be given a limited amount of time to raise money to bid to buy the asset as part of an open process. The right covers community facilities, such as shops, pubs, and community centres, and covers private as well as public assets.
- The 'Community Right to Build' allowed local communities to undertake small-scale, site-specific, community-led developments. The new powers gave communities the freedom to build new homes, shops, businesses, or facilities where they want them, without going through the normal planning application process.

These new rights gave local communities power over their elected councils, but they are not powers that strengthen the overall accountability of the elected council (and local councillors) to the community. Apart from the 'fatal ambiguity' that these provisions demonstrate about the dominant purpose of localism (see below), they and the regulations that accompany them involved an unwarranted centralist intrusion into the way in which local authorities deal with local communities. Relationships between local authorities and local communities are a field in which local authorities have infinitely more experience and knowledge than central government, and might reasonably expect to be trusted to use their own judgements, not least in understanding the diversity of community groups, and the variations in their representative legitimacy.

Little use has been made of these powers since the act's introduction in 2011. If the main intention of the act was to stimulate local community activity of this nature, it has failed to do so, in each of the three categories concerned.

Centralism is entrenched in the act by the plethora of new powers, regulations, and orders (or reaffirmations thereof) proposed for ministers to exercise. A better title would have been the 'Centralism Act'.

Local authority or local community-based localism?

There was a fatal ambiguity in the act that arose because of confusion about the meaning of localism. Was the act primarily about governmental localism — that is, localism for local authorities — or was it about localism for communities, which involves the allocation of powers that bypass the democratic processes of local authorities and that may indeed undermine them? There is a tension between devolution to local authorities and devolution to local communities, which was apparent in the ministerial speeches in the run up to the Localism Bill, and that was not resolved by the content of the act itself. Unless this relationship is clear and understood at the local level and at the centre, confusion and conflict between communities and local authorities would undermine aspirations for localism, whether to local government or communities.

If the main thrust of the government's vision of localism was in the direction of local communities (which with the benefit of hindsight appears highly likely), then what would be involved would be a further shift of power away from local government to less-accountable governmental bodies (previously QUANGOS, now amorphous 'community groups'). It would reflect a distrust of local government and a disdain for its lead role in the local-governance network. Local communities typically involve a mix of special interest groups, neighbourhood-based organisations, and influential individuals, raising issues about their accountability to local people. It is right that they should play an increasing role in the government of their areas, but only the local authority itself is in a position to channel and harness the aspirations and energies of such groups and individuals, and to balance different interests, in a local environment that it understands far better than do ministers and civil servants in Whitehall.

The missing participants in localism

If localism were to become a reality for local authorities, the project would have had to gain the commitment of other key departments of state (for

example, the Treasury, Education, Home Office, and Health) whose policies have always had a direct impact upon local authorities' powers and
scope for manoeuvre. The reality is that DCLG proved unable to persuade
other ministers in Whitehall to take localism seriously. This outcome is by
no means surprising. DCLG and its predecessors have never been 'big hitters'
(even when headed by Deputy Prime Minister John Prescott), either in
budget negotiations, or in their ability to exert much influence on behalf of
local government on other departments, where the spirit of centralism is
deeply entrenched. The main barriers to the development of localism lay in
central government itself, and localism would not develop its potential
unless there was a fundamental change in the working of central
government.

The absence of a finance dimension

There was a notable omission in the Localism Act: it did not deal with the
financing of local government. It was left to a later separate Resources
Review to address this issue, but it did so only by making proposals for
dealing with the business rate. The consultation paper produced by the
Resources Review offered local government a share of the business rate,
which the Secretary of State told the House of Commons 'was a way of
increasing local financial control and restoring councils' financial autonomy'. In reality, as Jones and Stewart (2011, p20) point out, 'far from being
a means of increasing local financial control and restoring financial autonomy, the main objective of the "repatriation" of business rates is to create a
substantial incentive for local authorities to drive central government's goal
of economic growth'. Neither this nor any of the other measures floated
begin to address the fundamental problem, which is the heavy reliance of
local authorities on centrally determined and regulated support-grants, and,
above all, the capping of the capacity of the taxation powers of local
authorities:

> There will be no genuine localism until the Government follows
> the approach of the 1976 Layfield Committee. The Layfield message
> was the need to reduce local government's dependence on high
> levels of central grants and an extension of local government's own
> tax base. Without such financial decentralisation centralism will
> prevail.
>
> *(Jones and Stewart 2011, p20)*

Education

Nowhere is the mismatch between DCLG's localism rhetoric and the actions of other departments more striking than in the Department for Education. For many years now there has been a steady process of erosion of local authorities' education responsibilities. Simon Jenkins (2012) makes the point forcefully:

> In the quarter century since Kenneth Baker began his great Whitehall power grab over the school system, ministers have striven for a nationalised education service, one to rival the mighty NHS. As a result, education authorities now have little or no discretion over school buildings and finance, pupil allocation, the teaching profession or the curriculum. Some now only have their primary schools.

This changing balance between central and local responsibilities, which has never been coherently justified by the centre as a strategic policy, has produced what is fast becoming a de facto national educational system.

There has developed a major anomaly between the increasingly limited scope for policy choice that local authorities now possess and the formal responsibility that they still nominally have for education (and the high, although diminishing, proportion of education expenditure in local-authority budgets). Logically, central government should either take formal responsibility for primary and secondary education, turning it into a 'national service' (which would negate the principle of 'subsidiarity' and fly in the face of any credible definition of 'localism'), or it should initiate a major switch of responsibilities and choice back to local authorities. In reality, neither outcome is likely to come about. Blame for failures in the education system can be attributed to councils by focusing on an obscure provision in the 2006 Act, which 'makes councils responsible for all state schools in their area, including those they do not run', while removing any power to enable them to discharge that responsibility. This device is an ingenious way for enabling the centre to demand the credit for success, but delegate the blame. It involves an unhelpful blurring of local and central responsibilities.

Before his sudden removal from office in 2014, the process of centralisation under the coalition government was insidiously accelerated by then Secretary of State for Education Michael Gove. Academies (and free schools), outside the effective influence of local government and without any medium of local accountability, came to account for almost half of all secondary schools. There has been growing central-government pressure on primary schools to opt for academy status, a move that has angered several councils under Conservative control, such as Lancashire. Under the 2015 Conservative government, the move to academies and free schools was set to gather further momentum, suggesting that it will not be long before a 'national education service' emerges, in all but name.

But with what justification? To quote Jenkins (2012) again:

> Central government takes credit for the academies that now embrace half of secondary schools. Though some have failed, those that replaced bad inner city schools have undeniably raised standards. Given the money and leadership hurled at them by Whitehall, this is hardly surprising, but the same might have been achieved had councils been given the same resources.

It might indeed. In a letter responding to Jenkins's article from the chair of Camden chairs and governors' forum (*The Guardian*, 30 November 2012), the case for local control over schools is powerfully made:

> Camden has now been recognised by Ofsted as having the best outcomes in the country … the 'Camden model' is based on the recognition that schools thrive not by making themselves independent of the local authority, but by being part of a 'family of schools' that works closely in partnership with the LEA; a partnership that is based on mutual challenge, not on control from the centre. In Camden, there are hardly any academies and free schools.

Councillor Peter Downes, in a letter to *The Guardian* (14 December 2012), set out a powerful critique of Michael Gove's educational reforms:

> His deliberate destruction of the local school system, where schools had been supported, challenged and coordinated by democratically-elected local authorities, has turned out to be divisive, unfair and costly. Divisive because academies and free schools are perceived to be brilliant, outstanding, inspirational, world-class etc (Gove is great on hyperbole) and local authority schools mediocre, unambitious and failing. Unfair because extra resources have been directed towards 'outstanding' schools, serving favoured catchment areas. Costly because in the two years 2010–2012, the academies programme overspent by £1 billion, as the recent National Audit Office report revealed.

It would be hard to find a more vivid example of the disdain with which ministers regard local government, and their readiness to introduce centralist policies that marginalise its role, than in the way academies and free schools have been introduced.

Before Kenneth Baker's 1988 Education Reform Act, the education secretary had just three powers over schools. Baker increased those powers to 250, but Michael Gove has now given himself more than 2000.

In state education, what took place under the coalition government was a process of rampant (rather than incremental) centralisation, with little in the way of philosophical or rational underpinning, resulting in an education system in which accountability has become increasingly diffuse. Michael Gove would no doubt argue that by 'freeing' schools from the shackles of local-authority control, he was contributing to localism. But, crucially, the funding of academies and free schools comes direct from the centre.

Policing and crime prevention

Throughout the 20th century all successive governments have recognised the case for some form of local accountability mechanism for police forces. In the 1975 local government reorganisation, Watch Committees were replaced by Police Committees on a county-by-county basis (including in the newly formed metropolitan counties). In some areas (such as West Mercia and Thames Valley), where the police force covered more than one county, there was a joint committee. Police Committees had a quota of co-opted magistrates, but local councillors were always in a majority (taking into account the casting vote of the chair). There was a recognition of a clear distinction between 'strategic' and 'operational' matters, and an acceptance on Police Committees (or Police Authorities, as they were known) that they needed to refrain from involvement in the latter. The system worked reasonably well as a mechanism for holding police forces to account. There were several forcefully expressed differences of opinion between police authorities and chief constables over controversial issues (for example, the miners' strike in 1984; Keith Oxford's handling of the Liverpool riots in 1981). Accountability of Police Authorities was weakened when it was decided that councillors should no longer hold a majority of seats.

In 2011 the coalition government decided to introduce a new indivi-dualistic form of accountability. Police Commissioners were to be elected in each police area, with powers to decide the local policing budget, to hire and fire chief constables, and to establish local strategies for dealing with crime and disorder. Elections were held in November 2012, and inspired a derisory voting turnout of 15 per cent on average. Most of the elected commissioners had a party political affiliation, although six or seven were Independents.

In reality, the Home Office had excluded local authorities by introducing this measure. During the August 2011 riots, 'it seemed as if policing was a central government responsibility, to be directed from Whitehall by the Home Secretary. Local authorities however, were to the fore in the clear-up' (Jones and Stewart 2011, p19).

Land-use planning

It is perhaps unsurprising that DCLG has failed to influence other central-government departments in seeking (if indeed it ever did) to broaden the scope of its localism project. Its previous record in influencing the Whitehall big-hitters has not been encouraging. But it would be reasonable to expect that the department would ensure that the principles of localism were applied to those local services, such as housing and planning, which fell within its remit. It was a test of the department's genuine commitment to the local-government dimension of localism that it should do so.

In fact, the localist credentials of DCLG do not look impressive when its 2011–2015 record is examined. Both planning and housing had previously experienced 30 years of centralisation, under governments that made no claims to be implementing a localist agenda (although the 1997–2001 Labour government made a number of gestures in this direction). Had DCLG sought to reverse this trend, on the basis of localist principles? There is little evidence that it did.

The decline, since the 1980s, in the status of town planning and the dilution of the devolvement that had previously underpinned its operation was noted in Chapter 2 and is explored in more detail as an illustration of the cumulative, albeit disjointed process of centralisation over the same period in Chapter 4. From 2010 to 2015, apart from dismantling the Labour-instigated regional-planning function, the coalition government did little to change the central dominance over planning, perpetrated by the previous Labour government. One of the most insidious impacts of the weakening of local choice in land-use planning has been the problems that local authorities face in refusing applications by supermarket chains, even where there is clear evidence that public opinion is opposed to them. Legally, a local authority can refuse such an application. But it knows that if Tesco or Asda appeals against the decision, as it is entitled to do (and has nothing to lose by so doing) and wins the appeal, then the local authority has to pay the costs of the appeal inquiry. Berwick-upon-Tweed was nearly bankrupted in the 1990s when its refusal of planning permission was overturned in just such circumstances.

The Localism Act did little to reverse these centralist trends. It contained provisions that reduce the amount of regulation from the top, placing powers in the hands of local communities to drive planning from below. However, any localist gains looked likely to be nullified by the secretary of state's proposed national planning framework, which embodies a strong presumption in favour of (so-called) sustainable development, with incentives for local authorities to agree to schemes of development (sustainable or otherwise). There is a strong implication here that developers will be given the opportunity to bypass local objections (Jones and Stewart 2011, p16).

Social housing

There was a time (1970–1980) when the three most high-profile services (in both status and expenditure) in urban authorities (Metropolitan and London boroughs) were education, social services, and housing. In each service, councils operated with a considerable degree of freedom from central edict or constraint. We have seen how that balance has changed drastically in education from 1987 onwards. Social services had not experienced the same level of central interference (although it has not escaped it). The main problem here is the increasing mismatch between resource availability and growing service demand, especially amongst the elderly. Social housing was the first of the 'big three' to find itself subjected to a major intervention from the centre. One of the first initiatives of the first Thatcher government was to introduce 'the right to buy' for tenants of council houses, at very favourable prices. This policy was introduced for party political reasons, in particular to break up the traditional solidity of Labour support on council estates, and to fulfil a longstanding Conservative commitment to create a property-owning democracy. Local authorities could have provided social housing to meet the level of need if they had been permitted to continue to build council houses. But they were not allowed to do so. The council-owned stock was progressively depleted by the 'right-to-buy' legislation, typically in the 'more desirable' council estates, leaving the council stock with an increasing proportion of hard-to-let properties in 'less desirable' areas (not too many takers for high-rise flats!).

Then in the 1990s big financial incentives were provided to local authorities to transfer their remaining council-house stock to 'arms-length' agencies (established by the council), which then broke the link between housing need and allocation policy (still with local authorities) and implementation (now with an arms-length agency). Despite a widespread expectation that the 1997 Labour government (and its successors) would re-introduce the role of councils as providers of new social housing, it did so only on a limited scale.

One of the outcomes of this removal of a well-established council responsibility has been a well-documented crisis in the availability of social housing. The empowerment of local authorities to build social housing to meet local housing need should in principle be an uncontroversial measure. Why should a democratically elected accountable council not be the lead agency in doing so? It is acknowledged that not all council housing departments were well-run, and that some developed rigid and inflexible approaches to council-house allocation. But all public agencies – central government, local government, and QUANGOS – have been vulnerable to sub-optimal management practices (see Chapter 4). The key question is whether, in principle, it is appropriate for councils to regain a lead role in the provision and allocation of social housing, particularly when the present set of arrangements is clearly not meeting the level of need, and a sense of crisis is increasingly pervading this crucial service.

Has the localism agenda done anything to empower local authorities to deal with this crisis? The answer is, on the surface it has, but in reality it hasn't. Jones and Stewart (2011, p16) argue that the threadbare nature of the government's commitment to localism was revealed in the CLG consultation paper *Implementing Self-Financing for Council Housing* (CLG 2011a) that lays down that borrowing by local authorities for housing is included in the Public Sector Borrowing Requirement. Whitehall will set a Council House Borrowing Requirement for each council. There will be no scope for a council to spend beyond this precise allocation, which is likely to fall well short of what the council would need to spend to make serious inroads into dealing with the problem.

There were other features of the Localism Act and other recent initiatives that sat uneasily with the spirit of localism. Although the switch of responsibility for public health from the NHS to local government was a welcome contribution to localism, this gain was balanced by the missed opportunity in not placing the commissioning of health care with local government. Instead this role has been allocated to consortia of general practitioners (GPs) and other professionals in Clinical Commissioning Groups. In other words, the spirit of centralism continues to pervade the new arrangements. It remains to be seen whether George Osborne's transfer of the NHS budget for the Greater Manchester area to the Greater Manchester Combined Authorities is the start of a genuine devolutionary trend in health, or was motivated by electoral considerations as the 2015 general election approached.

The responsibility for administering housing benefits has been transferred from central government (where it had formed part of the workload of local welfare benefits officers) to local authorities. This move raises an important point of principle as to whether it is appropriate for the centre to require the local authority to act as its administrative agent for a function where there is little or no scope for local choice. Such a move blurs accountability, a concern that was highlighted when, in 2012, a central-government decision was made to impose a cap on benefits payments. As a consequence, the level of housing benefit that local authorities were permitted to allocate to families was, in many cases, inadequate to cover the rent of the dwellings in which they lived. A further consequence was an increase in homelessness (particularly in London where rents are generally much higher than elsewhere), which in turn led local authorities, who were unable to deal with this problem within their own boundaries, to seek to identify affordable accommodation outside their boundaries, in some cases, a long distance away.

For a brief period in the late 1920s and early 1930s local authorities, having replaced the Poor Law Administrators, were empowered to set benefit levels to meet what they perceived as local need, before the function was nationalised in 1936. It would be unrealistic to expect a return of that power of flexibility over welfare-benefit payments at the present time. But what is equally inappropriate is to require local authorities to implement a centrally imposed benefits cap (for which they will no doubt be (mistakenly) held responsible by some of those affected) and then to deal with the resulting public opprobrium over matters they are in no position to rectify.

There is one local service where there has so far been little government predisposition for centralisation, namely child protection (although by 2016 in one or two authorities responsibility for this service had been switched to independent trusts). Despite ministers intervening in particular cases, such as Ed Balls's insistence that Sharon Shoesmith, then director of children's services in Haringey, should be dismissed following the 'Baby P' child-abuse tragedy (an edict subsequently found to be illegal), there is little evidence that the centre wishes to take over responsibility for this service. This attitude is hardly surprising; why would ministers want to take on responsibility for such 'risky' services vulnerable to 'bad news stories'? Following the 2015 general election, however, there have been introduced provisions for switching responsibility for child protection from authorities deemed to be 'failing' to other bodies, including charitable trusts, providing yet another development in the process of centralisation.

What is the overall verdict on the way in which the coalition dealt with local government over its five years in power? It has to be one of huge disappointment, particularly in the light of the flickers of hope contained in the Conservative Party's pre-election policy paper, and the positive signals (illusory, as it transpired) associated with the launch of 'localism'. In a sense, 'localism' and the Localism Act turned out to be a damp squib, especially in the way it was oversold (Eric Pickles announced his three main priorities at the 2010 Conservative Party conference as 'Localism, localism and localism'). Apart from providing some crumbs of empowerment to community groups (of which relatively little use has so far been made), the localism initiative has proved ineffective. In common with its bedfellow 'the big society', there is a profound disparity between the way in which they were presented as 'big ideas', and their ultimate impact: a case of a good deal of sound and fury signifying very little! The measures introduced under the banner of localism illustrate how limited was central government's understanding of the local circumstances and institutions in which they sought to intervene.

More significant in the pattern of central–local relations over the 2010–2015 period have been three other factors, all of which have had the effect of further marginalising the role of local government. First, there has been the financial straitjacket imposed on local councils throughout the period. Their lack of opportunity to pursue any strategy other than 'damage limitation' has arisen from a combination of the increasingly drastic year-by-year reductions in central-government grants, and the restrictions placed on their ability to compensate (even partially) as a result of the 2 per cent ceiling placed on council-tax increases throughout the period (this restriction could only be overturned following a positive response to a proposal in a local referendum, which has not been activated anywhere). Second, there was the lack of any tangible commitment by the other major Departments of State to the concept of localism (at least in as far as it involved local councils). The Department for Education, the Home Office, and the Treasury have all in their own ways pursued agendas that weakened rather than strengthened local government. Third, there was the lack of empathy with local government by Secretary of State Eric Pickles. Indeed, 'hostility' is a more accurate characterisation of his attitude; he appeared to view his mission as 'bashing local government', rather than acting as its advocate: a strange stance indeed for a secretary of state to adopt to the subject of his or her own department!

   The Localism Act can be interpreted in one of two ways: either as a cynical ploy to distract attention from the harshness of the cuts that the coalition knew from the start they would be imposing on local government, or as a 'big idea' that was never thought through in sufficient detail to enable it to make a real impact, and was subsequently marginalised by the dominant culture in other departments of state, which resisted any significant move to localism. The most likely interpretation of what happened is that in the inter-party discussions within the coalition in the aftermath of the 2010 election a commitment to localism was seen as helpful common ground between the Conservatives (who had trailed it in a pre-election policy paper) and the Liberal Democrats, who have long been confirmed localists. Where 'localism' would lead would then depend on the predispositions of the minister concerned, and the advice provided by the senior civil servants in the DCLG. Given the belligerent attitude to local government of the former, and the dismissive attitude of the latter, it is not surprising that the implementation of 'localism' not only failed to empower local authorities, but in practice contributed to increasing their marginalisation. This explanatory perspective is developed further in the next chapter. There is a parallel with the expectations of a reversal of centralisation and the revitalisation of local government that were widespread in the aftermath of Labour's 1997 election victory (see Chapter 2). The expectations were not fulfilled, and over the 13 years of Labour rule, the inexorable process of centralisation continued.

4

CENTRAL–LOCAL RELATIONS

An interpretation

Chapters 2 and 3 catalogued the cumulative decline in the powers and status of local government since 1979, leading in 2015 to a point where 'marginalisation' best describes the outcome. Before moving on in Part II of the book to a consideration of what roles and responsibilities might be allocated (or re-allocated) to local government when English devolution is taken forward, it is important that this chapter should explain how this process of marginalisation has come about. Has it been the result of a deliberate (if clandestine) strategy on the part of successive governments of differing political compositions? Or is it more convincingly explained as the outcome of a series of ad hoc measures by different ministers (including prime ministers) over the years? There is also the issue of whether the process of marginalisation, to whatever degree it has been deliberate, can be justified. Is there evidence that local government has proved significantly more incompetent and/or corrupt than its central counterpart, to an extent that the process of ever-increasing centralisation can be deemed to be necessary to protect the interests of citizens?

The idea that the cumulative erosion of local government's position has occurred because of a deliberate strategy shared between the two major parties would require a stronger belief in conspiracy theory than seems justifiable. Until the election in 1979 of a Conservative government led by Margaret Thatcher, the partnership model of central–local relations had prevailed, albeit with the occasional conflict over issues such as the sale of council houses (Clay Cross) or the implementation of comprehensive education (Tameside). Leadership of a local authority continued to be one of the key pathways to becoming an MP (and sometimes, in due course, ministerial office). The public reputation of local government, or more specifically, that of the manual workers within it, had declined as a consequence of the 1978–1979 'winter of discontent', but not to an irretrievable extent.

The main destabilising factor of the previous relatively benign climate of central–local relations was the juxtaposition of a prime minister, ideologically and personally antipathetic to local government, and the growing influence of the so-called 'hard left' in the town and county halls of Britain. The conflict between these two ideologies led directly or indirectly to a range of central-government initiatives – rate-capping, the abolition of the Greater London Council (GLC) and the six metropolitan county councils, and the introduction of compulsory competitive tendering – that in other circumstances would probably have not been felt to be necessary. The conflicts generating these measures and the responses to them reset the parameters of central–local relations, and launched them in a direction of centralisation that has continued ever since.

There was nothing inevitable about the continuation of this change of direction. It could have been reversed, had subsequent governments (or individuals in key ministerial positions) accepted the case for doing so. The influence of individuals has been important, although individual influence does not provide in itself a full explanation (see below). In many ways, local government has been unfortunate in the ministers it has had to deal with since 1979. Nicholas Ridley, appointed as secretary of state for the environment in 1987, was a committed neo-liberal with a distaste for the public sector, and for local government in particular, which matched that of his leader. Eric Pickles, appointed to the equivalent post in 2010, preferred a bombastic, demeaning approach to local government, rather than the more familiar ministerial ethos of supporting and speaking out for the service for which he had departmental responsibility. Ministers who held a more positive view, such as Chris Patten, Stephen Byers, and (possibly) David Miliband were never in post long enough to make much difference. At the prime ministerial level, neither Tony Blair nor John Major had particularly relished their brief involvement in local politics (the latter as an opposition councillor in the London Borough of Lambeth in the late 1960s), and neither Gordon Brown nor David Cameron appeared remotely interested.

The trajectory of central–local relations can be linked to a series of ad hoc issues, which individual ministers have either felt obliged to deal with, or have chosen to do so. Town planning provides a helpful example of the way in which the erosion of a local function has often proceeded in fits and starts, influenced by individual ministerial perspectives.

The centralisation of land-use planning

During the 1960s, land-use planning enjoyed an unprecedented growth surge, in both the scope of its responsibilities and its status. In 1965 the Planning Advisory Group (PAG) produced a report *The Future of Development Plans* that laid down a comprehensive planning framework, comprising structure plans, local plans, and development control (which was already an established feature of the local planning system, but would now be set in a clearer policy context). The lead role in these new arrangements lay clearly with local government, with the centre's involvement limited to providing contextual guidance, and appointing independent inspectors to examine structure and local plans at the draft stage. Land-use planning was justifiably seen as an activity for which local authorities should have the primary responsibility, unless an issue of demonstrable national interest (such as a defence establishment) was involved, a view that still prevails in most other Western democracies. In Britain, however, this devolutionary assumption has been eroded by a series of central-government interventions, which have over time transformed the central–local balance of power in favour of the former.

The first major disruption to this locality-led approach to planning came in the early 1980s. Michael Heseltine (the secretary of state for the environment) soon became frustrated with the inactivity of city councils (largely Labour-led, at the time) in stimulating local economic development. In his view, 'nothing was happening.' In 1980, he announced that two new Urban Development Corporations (UDCs), operating independently of the local authorities in which they were located, would be established in the East End of London and in Liverpool. Later in the year, a further nine UDCs were set up in other major provincial cities.

Within two or three years, city councils had begun to take a much more proactive approach to economic development, and with some success. But the precedent had been set. For the first time since the decision in 1946 to entrust the development of new towns to appointed boards rather than local authorities, the centre had usurped the responsibility of local authorities for land-use planning, in this case within large areas of the major cities.

The UDC initiative was soon followed by the setting up of Enterprise Zones, the brainchild of Chancellor of the Exchequer Geoffrey Howe. In

Enterprise Zones, development was permitted free of regulation, training levies, and liability for local rates. Again, local planning controls were by-passed, leading to 'disastrous visual and commercial consequences; the sites were grossly overdeveloped, and many firms swiftly became bankrupt' (Jenkins 1994, p160).

A further weakening of the local authority planning role followed when Heseltine unearthed an obscure power in the 1971 Planning Act that enabled him to make Special Development Orders, to 'stimulate development in acceptable locations and speed up the planning process', which turned out to be a mechanism to enable the centre to push through office devel-opments where local authorities were reluctant to agree to them, at the same time disregarding objections from local communities. The use of these orders, together with the other measures described above, made it clear that the statutory processes of land-use planning could be circumvented by a government pre-disposed to do so.

The second blow to the integrity and coherence of the PAG-based local planning system came in 1983 in the form of a Conservative manifesto commitment to abolish the GLC and the six metropolitan county councils. Although this controversial party-political measure was not in itself targeted at the land-use planning system, it had a disruptive effect on it, in the seven locations in England where the need for area-wide structure plans was strongest, not least because of the complexity of the land-use/transportation interrelationships involved. There was a bizarre and unsubstantiated reference in the distinctly sub standard White Paper *Streamlining the Cities* to 'a certain fashion for strategic planning which has proved exaggerated'. The reality was that the effect (and possibly one of the intentions) of the subsequent legislation was not to abolish strategic planning, but to centralise it. As Patrick Jenkin, the secretary of state at the time, acknowledged: 'there will remain the need for an overview of land-use planning issues in the metropo-litan areas. To meet this, I shall where necessary give planning guidance….to the boroughs and districts.' A further major shift towards the central domination of local-planning agendas was under way (Hansard 3 December 1994).

The hope that following its electoral success in 1997, Labour would reverse the centralising measures of its predecessor was as unfulfilled in relation to land-use planning as for other local-authority responsibilities. Worse than that, the 2004 Planning and Compulsory Purchase Act further depleted the powers of local planning authorities. In what Simon Jenkins (2004, p67) has described as 'the most serious Labour inroad into local democracy', the act stripped the county councils of any substantive land-use planning role.

Their structure planning, rural conservation, and economic development powers were transferred to the regional offices of John Prescott's own department (the Office of the Deputy Prime Minister, or ODPM). Prescott's long-held desire to establish regional government in the North-East had previously been unequivocally rejected in a referendum. But his enthusiasm for regionalisation continued, even in the absence of any democratic legitimacy in the regional decision-making machinery. The 2004 Act gave regional offices of the ODPM power to determine regional spatial strategies (subject to the approval of the Treasury), leaving little scope for any kind of strategic planning role beneath the regional level. Not only was the county councils' role drastically reduced, but district councils and unitary authorities were now required to prepare Local Development Frameworks, within the target-dominated guidelines of the regional strategies, including targets for new housing construction (on the basis of a disputed, demand-led methodology). Jenkins justifiably claims that the 2004 Act 'imposed central planning targets on the local planning framework to a degree unknown in England and unheard elsewhere in Europe' (2004, p67).

The 2012 Localism Act to some extent reduced the level of central regulation of planning. The new National Planning Policy Framework (NPPF) simplified national policy guidance. But other planning-related elements of the Act give grounds for concern. As noted in Chapter 3, the Coalition government's concept of localism was focused less on local authorities per se than on strengthening the powers of local communities to 'drive planning from below'. One of the new rights allocated to local communities is the 'Community Right to Build', which gives community organisations freedom to build new houses, shops, businesses, or facilities without going through the normal planning-application process. While measures to empower local communities are, in principle, to be welcomed, it should be recognised that such communities are rarely homogenous entities, but are normally composed of different groupings (or sub-communities), with different interests and priorities. One of the important attributes of a local authority is its legitimate democratic mandate to compare, balance, and respond to these competing agendas, on the basis of some broader conception of the public interest. Development control often throws up such up difficult choices; for example, the decision of an Asian community group to build a mosque in an area of mixed ethnicity, without needing to seek planning permission, would be likely to generate local controversy.

Second, there was the 'presumption in favour of sustainable development' which was included in the NPPF. There is ambiguity in the meaning attached to 'sustainable', but it appears that it is less concerned with ecological or environmental sustainability than it is with developments that create jobs and wealth, including new housing schemes. One former planning officer told Steve Leach that, in his view, 'the planning system is being dismantled behind the façade of the NPPF'.

This view is shared by Simon Jenkins (2013), who argues that, for the first time, national planning policy has 'enshrined profitability as a planning consideration, buried in such euphemisms as viability'. On balance, despite the simplification of national guidance, the provisions of the Localism Act have further eroded the role of local planning authorities.

We have demonstrated that the process of centralisation in land-use planning has proceeded in a piecemeal fashion over the past 40 or so years through a series of ad hoc governmental (or, more often, ministerial) initiatives, rather than as a long-term conscious strategy by the centre. There is little scope for conspiracy theories, although none of the successive governments have chosen to reverse the centralising measures of their predecessors. All of the key changes discussed here have been associated with particular individuals: Michael Heseltine for UDCs and SDOs; Geoffrey Howe for Enterprise Zones; Margaret Thatcher for the abolition of the GLC and the six metropolitan counties (widely regarded as an act of political vindictiveness directed at the Ken Livingstone-led regime at the GLC); John Prescott for the regionalisation of strategic planning; and Eric Pickles for the centralising provisions of the Localism Act. There is an element of 'historical accident' involved here; if different individuals had headed the Department of Environment (and its successors) then the pattern and perhaps direction of centralisation may well have been different. Usually, land-use planning has not proved a topic of high political salience. Within the constraints of manifesto commitments, much has been left to the discretion of individual ministers who may have been influenced by their civil servants, with prime ministers becoming involved only in exceptional circumstances. Of the various initiatives that have weakened land-use planning only one – the abolition of the GLC – bore the imprint of a prime minister. There is no evidence that David Cameron was interested enough in the subject to intervene in the initiatives introduced by Eric Pickles.

This pattern whereby local responsibilities have come to be progressively eroded by policy initiatives set in motion by individual ministers of state has also been apparent in other fields of governmental activity. The weakening of the local-authority role in education owes much to the predilections of Kenneth Baker (Con), David Blunkett (Lab), and (in particular) Michael

Gove (Con), who was left very much to his own devices by David Cameron and his cabinet colleagues. The current council-tax regime emerged in the wake of a convoluted series of changes (under different ministers) in attempts to control local expenditure, from rate-capping to the introduction of the community charge/poll tax (the original version of which would, ironically, have made local authorities much less reliant on central grant than they were before or have been since). Local government reorganisation initiatives from the Labour Secretary of State Peter Shore's 1979 'Organic Change' proposal through to the launch by Ruth Kelly (Lab) launch of the chaotic 2006–2008 'bidding for unitary status' exercise have all borne the stamp of ministerial preference (in the latter case, heavily influenced, one suspects, by civil servants). Elected mayors were a personal commitment by Michael Heseltine (Conservative), later to be taken up by Hilary Armstrong (Labour), David Cameron (Conservative), and (latterly) George Osborne (Conservative).

The role of changing assumptive worlds in Whitehall and Westminster

An analysis of centralisation that relies on the cumulative impact of an ad hoc series of disconnected ministerial initiatives is not in itself an adequate explanation. Unless there was some more deep-seated antipathy to local government that had percolated into the mind-sets of civil servants and ministers from 1979 onwards, one might expect that measures that diminished the powers of local government would have been balanced by measures that enhanced them. In fact it is difficult to identify more than one or two enhancing measures in the 1979–2015 period. The introduction of a power of general competence in the 2000 Local Government Act, the transfer of public-health responsibilities from the NHS back to local government in 2009, and the allocation of responsibilities for social care to local authorities (now under threat) in the mid-1990s are rare exceptions. The general picture is one of muddle, confusion, and internal departmental struggles within Whitehall.

There is, however, an important feature of the Whitehall culture that has provided a context within which different disempowering measures can be introduced, with little concern or challenge, and that is the assumptive world that now appears to dominate the attitudes of ministers and civil servants alike: the often tacit, unconsidered but widely shared way in which local government is perceived by ministers and mandarins alike. Until the end of the 1970s, there was little evidence of hostile or dismissive attitudes to local government by either. As Jones and Travers (1997) noted, 'continuous expansion of local authority expenditure in the period from the 1950s to 1975 had ensured that (by the standards of the mid-1980s) the relationship between local and central government was relatively smooth'. Even in the wake of the restrictions on public expenditure imposed by the International Monetary Fund (IMF) in 1975, local authorities had, in overall terms, delivered the savings expected of them by central government (see Jones and Stewart 1983). Civil servants may well have seen themselves as intellectually superior to the town and county clerks of the time (chief executives were then only just beginning to emerge), and to some (but by no means all) of the local-authority leaders they had to deal with, but there was no sense of the dismissive attitudes that Jones and Travers identified in 1994.

In 1979, a significant proportion of MPs, and some ministers, had been elected to parliament after a spell in a leadership position in a local authority, and hence would be likely to have some understanding and empathy with a world they had themselves experienced. There was also at that time a set of interactive central–local networks (professional, political, and managerial) linking central and local government, with the regional offices of the Departments of Environment and Transport acting as intermediaries. So what has changed since?

George Jones and Tony Travers, in their study of attitudes to local government in Westminster and Whitehall (Commission for Local Democracy 1994) provide some clues. Writing when the Conservatives had been in power for 15 years and the shrill anti-local government rhetoric of Margaret Thatcher had been replaced by the more emollient attitude of John Major, they discovered a mixture of ignorance and superiority regarding local government by senior civil servants:

> A gap of understanding exists between central and local government, much of which appears to be based on simple ignorance (or worse still, mistaken, stereotyped views). Civil servants appear, in some cases, to have little understanding of what local members and officers actually do … and appear to have little or nothing directly to do with them, even in departments whose services are run through local government.
>
> *(ibid, p16)*

There is little in the way of understanding or sympathy for the world of local government displayed here. The ministers interviewed for the study were somewhat less patronising and more sympathetic, but only to a degree. Indeed, one ministerial respondent held the following view:

> Local government is a lower middle-class activity, of course with some exceptions. The top mandarins of the civil service come from different social strata from those in local government … these differences point to differences in quality … Local government people have limited vision. There are some pretty good officers, but a lot are pretty ordinary.

Other ministers (probably those with local-government experience) spoke more positively and knowledgably about local government. But the general impression formed on reading Jones and Travers's paper is of a toxic blend of ignorance, superiority, and disparagement in the corridors of Whitehall and Westminster.

Central perceptions had changed since the partnership-dominated ethos of the 1970s (although the sense of superiority by both ministers and civil servants was probably present even then, although in a more tacit form). Given the ways in which civil servants pick up cues from their political masters (except where they are firmly opposed to them), what is likely to have happened is that the hostile attitudes of Margaret Thatcher, Nicholas Ridley, Kenneth Baker, and others had percolated into the assumptive worlds of civil servants, who had by 1994 collectively developed a mind-set that reflected these attitudes of disparagement and superiority. Had the 1997–2001 Labour government and its successors been committed to reversing the tide of centralisation, then a shift in the content of the assumptive worlds of senior civil servants would have been likely to follow. But revitalising local government was not seen as part of the New Labour project. As noted in Chapter 2, most of the changes introduced from 1997 to 2010 were changes in structures and processes (for example, elected mayors, local executives, and 'best value' and strategic partnerships) rather than the restoration of at least some of the powers removed in the previous Conservative era. There was little from New Labour that would have challenged the preconceptions that had come to dominate during the 1979–1997 period.

Mark Roberts (2016) uses the idea of 'narratives' to explain the process we have described. Narratives are sequences of events, experiences or actions with a plot which ties together different parts into a meaningful whole. A single narrative comprises of several 'embedded stories', which together support and exemplify the 'grand conception' of the narrative itself. Roberts argues that the concept of 'narratives' can be used to demonstrate how particular sets of ideas become taken for granted, and how politicians and civil servants are both consciously and unconsciously constrained by the normative elements ('should do'/'shouldn't do'). Narratives are not objective or neutral; on the contrary they express values and define power relationships. Roberts draws a comparison between central narratives relating to the National Health Service (NHS) and to local government, respectively, and argues that the long-running and deeply embedded political narrative about the NHS extols its moral virtues and concludes with the moral imperative that it would be political suicide to attempt to attack or dismantle this 'national treasure'. In the general election of 2010, all the major parties accepted that although draconian cuts to public services would be required to deal with the 'national debt crisis', the NHS should be protected, which remained the policy of the coalition government once it was elected, at the cost of correspondingly severe cuts in other public services. The general election of 2015 repeated the same pattern.

Roberts argues that what we are seeing here is a combination of conscious action and taken-for-granted ways of thinking that have become locked into what many would regard as a 'virtuous circle'. Using the same framework for analysis, he argues that a 'vicious circle' has developed from narratives of local government that invite citizens to disown and criticise their local administrations, and justify central government actors in policing and forcing changes upon them. In this way, the enduring power and stability of the narrative helps to explain why, when government changes hands, the attitudes and actions of those at the centre remain largely the same, and why we have seen a continuation of the hostility and contempt through Conservative, New Labour, and Coalition administrations since the 1980s, despite the discontinuity of actors at both levels.

Certain attitudes frequently crop up in the assumptive worlds of both ministers and civil servants that contribute to this narrative:

- Private-sector provision is superior to public sector provision.
- Management of the economy requires central control of the total of local-government expenditure, even if it is financed by local taxation, and not just the level of government grant allocated.
- Schools need to be freed from local-authority control if educational standards are to be improved.

- Only a marginal contribution to the demand for social housing should be made by new council housing.
- Large unitary authorities are more efficient and effective than two-tier local government.
- The calibre of local councillors is poor and in decline.
- Effective local leadership is best secured by directly elected mayors.

All these beliefs can and should be challenged, which we do in Part II of this book. They comprise a resilient set of so-called 'common sense' perspectives, so widely shared in Westminster and Whitehall that anyone who disagrees with them is viewed with incredulity. There is some comfort to be gained from an awareness that 'ideas in good currency' are vulnerable to change over time. As Owen Jones (2014) points out, the neo-liberal nexus of values that came to dominate the thinking of the Thatcher governments were for many years previously seen as 'beyond the pale'. We should not assume that they will not in time be overturned by a different ideology, one more sympathetic to the importance of strong local government in a unitary state.

Finally, we need to address the issues of corruption and competence. Is there any evidence that centralisation can be justified in the public interest because incompetence and corruption are more prevalent in local than in central government? Some elements in the centre's 'local government narrative' imply that there is a difference, with local government performing worse in both respects. For several decades, central government ministers and civil servants, aided by the media, have selectively identified and embellished accounts of local government practice that consolidate pre-judicial narratives in the public mind. There are several examples. The 'rotten borough' narrative portrays local government as corrupt, whether it is fixing the vote, giving jobs to friends and relatives, or taking bribes for planning permissions. The 'dangerously incompetent council' has a range of different storylines, but has tended to focus since the 1980s on child-protection scandals. The 'bureaucracy gone mad' narrative can relate to any public-sector body, but has been applied to local authorities, particularly over 'health and safety' stories, dealing, for example, with the felling of trees in residential areas. Finally, there is the 'stick-in-the-mud' narrative, portraying councils as reluctant to accept the case for change, and as demonstrating a reluctance to innovate, often contrasted with the flexibility and inventiveness of the private sector (see Roberts 2016).

The hypocrisy of central government's position is apparent on three counts. Its own record of incompetence and corruption is far from exemplary, and indeed often exceeds that of local government in its scope. All public (and, indeed, private and voluntary) organisations are vulnerable to incompetence, occasional performance failure, and corruption. Second, central government has often adopted local authorities' good practice and innovation, with little acknowledgement of its indebtedness to its junior partner. Third, because local government is a direct provider of services, and central government (with very few exceptions) is not, it is inevitable that the former will be more vulnerable to performance failures involving human suffering (such as failure to spot serious cases of child abuse) than the latter.

With corruption, there have been a number of high-profile examples from local government, including Newcastle's leader in the 1960s T. Dan Smith (personal corruption), and, more recently, the suspension of the elected mayor of Tower Hamlets as a result of accusations of vote-rigging, later proven. But central government can provide a 'rogues gallery' of greater notoriety. Reginald Maudling was forced to resign in 1972, following his entanglement in the John Poulson's web of corruption. The 1970s also saw the 'Lavender List' of honours during Harold Wilson's premiership. In the 1990s, Neil Hamilton's case began a series of 'cash for questions' scandals, while 2010 saw three former Labour cabinet ministers, Stephen Byers, Patricia Hewitt, and Geoff Hoon, offering to use their insider contacts to influence government policy in return for cash. The 'MPs Expenses' scandal ran from 2009 through to 2011, and, in resignations, de-selections, criminal charges, and jail sentences indicated corruption on an unprecedented scale. It is impossible to make a convincing case that local government has proved more corrupt than its central counterpart; if anything, the reverse is true.

With 'incompetence and performance failure', the record of local government is sprinkled with shortcomings. There has been rigid and insensitive management of (some) council estates, the inefficiency and lack of customer care of (some) Direct Labour Organisations, the high-profile failures of child protection (Maria Colwell, Jasmine Beckford, Victoria Climbie, and Peter Connelly) and the abuse discovered in care homes for both children and frail older people. But if anyone doubts that central government has an array of skeletons in the cupboard, a scan through the pages of Anthony King and Ivor Crewe's *The Blunders of our Government* (2016) will quickly convince them otherwise. The fiascos of the Child Support Agency, the Asset Recovery Agency, and Individual Learning Accounts, the millions of pounds wasted on the public–private partnership to maintain and upgrade the London Underground system, and, of course, the introduction and then the retreat from the poll tax all bear testament to a level of governmental incompetence that overshadows local government's record.

Local government has a long record of successful policy innovation (as well as occasional and inevitable policy failures). Consider, for example, the imaginative attempts by many local authorities in the late 1970s and 1980s to revive their local economies, embracing town-centre regeneration, support for small firms, business promotion, tourism, and the establishment of co-operatives. Or the success in greatly increasing the proportion of children in local-authority care who were found foster parents (25 per cent in 1972 to 68 per cent in 2003). Local authorities led the way in embedding racial-equality policies and practices into their ways of working, often, in the 1980s, in the face of considerable opposition from central government and the media. And there is little that central government can teach local authorities about devolving local services and governance arrangements to local neighbourhoods and communities. In their different ways, Tower Hamlets, Walsall, Islington, and Birmingham (and many others) have proved pioneers in such devolution initiatives, ever since the early 1980s.

In the process of carrying out such innovation, local authorities have often identified deficiencies in national policy, and have introduced or lobbied for improvements long before the machinery of state has ground into action. This state of affairs is hardly surprising, when it is recognised there is greater capacity for innovation and learning among about 400 local councils, compared with a single central government establishment, which has learned a great deal from its local counterparts over the years, but has rarely acknowledged its debt or apportioned credit where it was due.

Is change possible?

Objections to our view of local government and its potential and to our proposals for a way ahead usually argue that they will never happen because of politics. But this view is short-sighted. Jones (2014) highlights the eventual success of Madsen Pirie and his fellow neo-liberalist travellers in helping to 'shift the goalposts of debate in Britain, making ideas that were once thought ludicrous, absurd and wacky become the new common sense'.

The current establishment view of local government, which seeks to dilute or remove its responsibilities, and which embraces a series of critical 'of course statements' needs to be confronted and reversed. A successful challenge, and a further move of the goalposts (in the reverse direction) is essential if local government is to be revived and to rediscover its lost role and status. For a start, local government itself, through its collective organisations, must challenge the centre much more forcibly than it has so far done, and advocate the kind of changes proposed in this book.

Part II of this book subjects the components of the current dominant narrative to critical scrutiny, and argues for a re-examination of conventional wisdom in the critical areas of constitutional protection, local finance, service responsibilities, territorial structure, and political-management arrangements, in a way that we hope will make a substantive contribution in the window of opportunity provided by the commitment to some form of devolution within England.

PART II

Moving forward

5

THE NEED FOR CONSTITUTIONAL CHANGE

Local government in Britain has always operated in a constitutional vacuum. Unlike all of its European neighbours (and, indeed, further afield), the United Kingdom does not possess a formal written constitution. This absence has had two important impacts upon local government. First, it has meant that there has been nothing to prevent central government from interfering with the way in which local authorities are designated, structured, and managed (including the responsibilities and duties that are allocated to or withdrawn from them). Second, it has caused a lack of clarity in the principles that should underpin their functions and responsibilities, which in turn makes it more difficult for central interference to be challenged. This chapter explores these two inter-related issues in depth, and develops proposals for change that would strengthen local government's constitutional position, and provide a better basis for deciding how responsibilities should be allocated between centre and locality, and how any changes therein should be managed.

There have been times in the history of central–local relations when the lack of a constitutional settlement (or anything approximating to it) has not appeared to be a problem. During the 30 years that followed the end of World War II, there existed a broad consensus between centre and local government about desired service developments (see Chapter 2). The goals of post-war reconstruction were shared. Local authorities were trusted to get on with the job of slum clearance, council-house construction, dealing with increasing car ownership and traffic congestion. Central government set out broad parameters for services such as education, child protection, and care of the elderly, and local authorities operated with considerable discretion delivering such services. At the time there were shared assumptions about central–local relations, which meant that issues were rarely raised about the appropriate roles and responsibilities of local government. Who needed a constitution?

This consensus was facilitated by the 'one nation' political ethos at national level, epitomised by the term 'Butskellism' (a reference to the similar economic philosophies of successive Labour and Conservative chancellors of the time). The consensus began to break down in the 1970s, and by the time the Conservatives, led by Margaret Thatcher, came to power in 1979, national politics had developed a more adversarial flavour. In such circumstances the consequences of the lack of a constitutional framework became more apparent, triggered by acts of central interference that had been largely absent in the previous 30 years.

Some of these measures would have been impossible without careful analysis and wide-ranging discussion in countries where the rights of local government are enshrined in a written constitution. Examples include the abolition of the Greater London Council (GLC) and the six metropolitan county councils in 1986, and the numerous ill-considered further reforms of local government structure that a partisan initiative had set in train, including the bizarre bidding system for unitary status introduced by the Labour government in 2006 (see Chisholm and Leach 2008). Local authorities were abolished and new ones established with a minimum of evidence-based justification. Other recent examples include the central government-imposed dismissal of Sharon Shoesmith, head of Childrens Services in the London Borough of Haringey, in the wake of the high-profile death of 'Baby P' in 2007 (a move later found to be illegal), and the attempt by Eric Pickles in 2013 to require all authorities in 2012 to carry out weekly refuse collections. Such examples have highlighted the ease with which central government can ultimately do what it pleases to local government, even down to arguably trivial detail.

The adoption by the 1997–2001 Labour government of the European Charter of Local Self-Government has been little help (although much of its content is admirable), because it was given no statutory backing. Similarly, the Concordat negotiated between central government and the Local Government Association in 2007 proved singularly ineffective in regulating central–local relations. Few civil servants outside the Department for Communities and Local Government (DCLG) were even aware of it, as shown when they gave evidence to a select committee. Although there is no immediate prospect of the United Kingdom adopting a written constitution, the idea of some form of quasi-constitutional settlement or statutory agreement, which would incorporate clear and wide-ranging principles to regulate central–local relations and that the current or any future government could not summarily opt out of, is sorely needed, and is a more realistic political possibility.

The two key questions that follow from this initiative are first how should it be taken forward, and, second, what principles should it include? Until the mid-1970s such a topic would have been seen as tailor-made for consideration by a Royal Commission. But Royal Commissions, however strong in principle the case for one is, have long since gone out of fashion, and despite their exemplary thoroughness in amassing evidence, they have the disadvantage of taking a long time. The need to achieve some form of constitutional settlement for local government requires a process that can be agreed and implemented with a greater degree of urgency, as part of the all-party commitment to devolution. The most promising way forward is by the introduction of a quasi-constitutional statute – through a code embodied in a statute. A statute would command attention in central-government departments, and, if it still remained a subject of contention, in the courts, too. Its formation would require an independent commission or committee, working to a specified limited time-scale, to agree its content after taking evidence from a range of relevant central and local interests. Some form of 'watchdog' mechanism would also be needed, to ensure that the principles contained within it were being appropriately applied.

Two such mechanisms were proposed by the Communities and Local Government Select Committee in its 2009 report *The Balance of Power: Central and Local Government*. It recommended the establishment of a unit at the heart of central government – possibly within the cabinet office – that would have the responsibility of monitoring whether the principles set out in the code were being embodied in government policies, and of overseeing whether actions taken by individual departments were or were not consistent with them. In addition, it proposed the setting up of a joint committee of both houses of parliament to monitor the application of the agreed principles, reporting annually to parliament on the relationship between central and local government, and on specific proposals, judging them against the requirements of the statutory code. These two proposals provide a requisite safeguard that the code would be taken seriously, whilst avoiding the dangers of over-elaboration.

What provisions should the statute contain? The principles set out below draw on the framework of the European Charter of Local Self-Government, but go beyond it, because the charter is over-cautious, as a result of a series of amendments sought in the original version by the then Conservative government. We set out below a series of proposals that would challenge the concept of the 'unitary state' by recognising and embodying in statute the democratic value of a local level of government, with a degree of autonomy that would provide a safeguard against the insidious process of centralisation that has characterised the past 30 or so years of central-government relations. Also set out is a basis for devolution, which would lead logically to a reversal of many of the changes in the balance of power between the two levels that had taken place over this period. As noted in Chapter 4, the relationship has changed gradually, without any deliberate and considered decision to do so, or even an awareness by the centre of the scale of the change that has gradually developed. It has happened step-by-step, as departments have put forward and secured agreement for proposals, all promoted on the basis of departmental merits, with no consideration of the cumulative impact of all the changes on the role of local government within the wider polity.

The proposed content of the code is set out under seven headings: the concept of local government; its scope; the protection of its boundaries; appropriate management structures; external supervision; financial resources; legislative powers and legal protection.

The meaning of local government

The first principle to emphasise, as we have throughout the book, is that the term 'local government' should mean what it says. The increasing use of the term 'local governance' since the late 1990s confuses rather than clarifies. The local-governmental role involves reviewing the whole range of local needs, problems, and priorities, and responding to them through local choice in an integrated fashion. This response will include the provision (directly or indirectly) of a range of local services, some of which may be legitimately shaped or constrained by central policies and priorities. But service provision is not in itself the raison d'être of local government. It is one of the means, which also include planning, regulation, influence, and advocacy, of furthering the well-being (economic, social, environmental, and cultural) of the local population, a principle that is echoed by the European Charter of Local Self-Government.

1 The primary role of local government, exercised by local elected councils, is the government of local communities, enabling their well-being.

The second principle refers to the way in which local government is funded. To exercise local choice in a meaningful way, local authorities need far more financial autonomy and flexibility than they enjoy at present. The most appropriate means of controlling local expenditure is the local election, not a central-government edict. It may be appropriate, as it has been in the not-too-distant past, for a central-government grant to be distributed in a way that compensates for significant differences in the level of need in different authorities, and for a similar degree of variation in the capacity to raise resources locally – currently, through council tax. The more the system of local-government finance can be built on locally raised resources the better. And linked to a greater degree of financial autonomy, there should be the power to deploy such resources in a way that maximises local well-being.

2 Local government needs the powers and resources under its own responsibility to carry out its primary governmental role.

It often appears that central government regards the primary accountability of local authorities as being to central government itself, rather than to their own citizens. This misconception has developed because of the increased reliance over the years of local authorities on central-government grants, and the constraints placed on both their overall levels of expenditure (through council-tax capping) and the way they spend their budgets. But this perspective is inappropriate; it is only relevant if local government is seen as the agent of the centre, which would undermine any possibility of genuine local government, as advocated in this book. In principle, the primary responsibility of local authorities should be to their local citizens, who are in a position to make judgements on the exercise of these responsibilities at and between local elections.

3 The primary accountability of local authorities for the exercise of their responsibilities is to their local citizens.

Scope of local government

Because there is currently no agreed statement of what the duties and powers of local authorities are (or should be), it is relatively easy for the centre to make changes in such duties and powers, as indeed they increasingly have done, without having to justify such changes against established criteria. In these circumstances 'cumulative centralisation' has taken place, where central governments do not have to justify their interventions. This anomaly can and should be remedied in the proposed code.

4 The basic duties and powers of local authorities should be prescribed by statute.

In deciding the scope of the duties and responsibilities of local government, the principle of subsidiarity should be the key reference point. The result of the recent referendum, which involved Britain detaching itself from the European Union (EU), provides a useful precedent here. The Brexit argument was (amongst other things) concerned with the devolution of powers from Brussels to the UK, a belief that powers and responsibilities were better exercised at this more local level. The same principle is equally relevant to the devolution of powers from central government to the four countries that make up the UK, and within England to the local-government level. The principle of subsidiarity requires that public responsibilities should be exercised by those authorities closest to the citizen. Thus, in a two-tier local-government system, the onus is on the county to make a case as to why a particular function needs to be exercised at the county rather than the district level. There will be examples where such an argument can be justified (for example, land-use and transportation planning, waste disposal, and policing), just as there will be some central-government functions that cannot sensibly be devolved to local authorities (for example, defence and counter-terrorism). But it is important that in every case the argument is made and, where possible, mutually accepted.

Subsidiarity further implies a readiness by local authorities to devolve responsibilities, where appropriate to grassroots bodies, not just town and parish councils, but area committees, tenant associations, and representative community organisations. Local authorities, not central government, should have the responsibility for developing the involvement and empowerment of their sub-local communities and citizens in public affairs. Local authorities understand much better than the centre the complex world of citizen involvement, including the capacity to judge how genuinely representative local-community organisations really are of their local communities. One of the problems with the 2010–2015 coalition government's localist agenda and legislation was their failure to recognise this capacity, and its related reluctance to place local authorities at the centre of the localism project, despite their legitimacy, as directly elected bodies, to play a lead role in the process.

At the centre of the reluctance of central government to allocate or restore powers and duties to local government was and is a concern with the so-called 'post-code lottery'. It is important to address the viability of the objection to a post-code lottery, as it has major implications for the central–local division of responsibilities. We do so later in this chapter.

The further principles that should be included in the code, on the basis of the arguments set out above, are listed below.

5 Public responsibilities should be exercised by elected authorities closest to citizens.

6 Local authorities should have the responsibility for developing the involvement and empowerment of their communities and citizens in public affairs.

One of the few positive moves in the direction of greater local autonomy has been the granting of a power of general competence to local authorities, incorporating the right to do anything that is within the law to improve the economic, social, and environmental well-being of their areas. This power has been relatively little used in the years of austerity that followed the financial crash of 2008. It is important that it should be emphasised in the code; it is a crucial tool in enabling local authorities to act in a governmental capacity. There is a related principle that focuses on the concept of community leadership. There are many other public-sector organisations within the boundaries of each local authority. In pursuing their governmental role it is appropriate that local authorities should have an acknowledged leadership role over such bodies, with powers to ensure that leadership is effective. Much has been made of the importance of elected mayors taking on this role, but such leadership should be a basic role for all local authorities, including the 95 per cent that do not operate with an elected mayor.

7 Local authorities should have full discretion to exercise their initiative on any matter not assigned by statute to any other public authority.

8 Local authorities should provide leadership to public bodies in their areas, based on their electoral mandate.

Protection of local-authority boundaries

One of the most counterproductive consequences of the lack of any constitutional protection for local authorities has been their vulnerability to the inclination of central government to make changes in the territorial structure of local government, in circumstances that typically reflect party-political considerations (for example, the abolition of the GLC and the six metropolitan county councils in 1986), rather than any rational analysis of the structural implications of social and economic change, or concern for the views of local citizens. In countries with a constitution that safeguards the rights of local authorities, such arbitrary intervention would not be possible. It should not be possible in the UK. There are circumstances in which changing social and economic patterns of life may call into question the appropriateness of the existing local government structure, as in the 1950s and 1960s when increasing car ownership and journey-to-work patterns justifiably led to the setting up of the GLC and the six metropolitan county councils. But if a change of this magnitude is contemplated, it should be investigated first by an independent inquiry, and not based on political convenience or ministerial whim.

9 Changes in the territorial structure of local government should not be possible without the involvement of an independent commission.

Appropriate management structures

One of the most controversial aspects of the 2015–2016 'devolution' initiative has been the insistence of the government that groups of authorities wishing to extract maximum benefit from a Combined Authorities initiative bid must accept a requirement to have a directly elected mayor. This obligation is the first example of a government insisting on this form of political leadership in local government, although from 2000 onwards, it has been clear that this political structure was central government's favoured option. We see no justification for the imposition of any such option on local authorities. Let them choose the type of political management that best suits their circumstances (which are bound to differ between a shire county, a small rural shire district, and a large city), whether a return to the committee system, cabinet government, or, indeed, a directly elected mayor. The same argument for not imposing structures from the centre should apply to management posts within local authorities. Why is it necessary for authorities to appoint a director of children's services if they prefer a different structural option, so long as the responsibilities involved are carried out effectively?

10 Local authorities should be able to determine their own internal political and management structures.

External supervision

From 1979 onwards the involvement of the centre in detailed scrutiny of the performance of local authority services increased substantially. Previously there were inspectorates for individual services, such as police, fire, education, and social services, but they played a more focused role than they have since (consider, for example, the comprehensive coverage of Ofsted, compared with the role of its predecessor, HM Inspector of Schools). Detailed scrutiny reached its peak in the work of the Audit Commission, which was then disbanded early in the 2010–2015 coalition government. But there remains a great deal of unnecessary supervision and subsequent direction of local government services by the centre. The danger is that central government regards such scrutiny as giving expression to inspectoral infallibility, without recognising that inspectors have their (often limited and partial) concepts of what constitutes 'good practice'. It would be appropriate for the code to include a principle regulating this unstructured set of central interventions.

There are two circumstances in which central intervention would be justified. First, if there were reasonable grounds for suspecting that a local authority was not complying with the law, such action would be justified. Second, if there were clear evidence of an unacceptable performance failure by part of a local council, that too might justify central intervention (the failures of child-safeguarding policy in Rotherham provide one recent example). But who decides what constitutes performance failure? There should be a set of guidelines, agreed between central and local government (represented by the LGA?), setting out the criteria on which performance failure could be identified, and hence central intervention justified. It should also be open to local authorities to initiate external inspection or assessment, in circumstances where they felt that it was required, or would be helpful, to be carried out by peer groups under the auspices of the LGA.

11 External supervision or inspection of the activities of local authorities should be initiated only to ensure compliance with the law, or in the light of evidence of performance failure, identified on the basis of mutually agreed criteria.

Financial resources

The question of how local government should be financed has a long and complex history, which is littered with unresolved inconsistencies, and unintended consequences of specific government policies – for example, in the aftermath of the introduction of the community charge/poll tax. The design of a system of local-government finance that supports the governmental role described in Principle 1 (above) is crucial for the ability of local authorities to play that role effectively. For this reason, we devote a separate chapter to the topic, following this one, which elaborates upon and develops the two basic principles set out immediately below, which should be included in the code.

12 Local authorities should be entitled to adequate financial resources of their own, which they should be able to deploy freely within the framework of their statutory powers.

13 All of the financial resources of local authorities should be derived from local taxes and charges over which they have the power to determine the rate. The only exceptions should be grants designed to correct the effects of the unequal distribution of potential sources of local finance, and of the financial burdens they support.

Legal protection

The statutory, quasi-constitutional, safeguarding of local authorities needs to be underpinned by some form of legal safeguarding, which protects them from any perceived breach of their statutory rights emanating from the centre.

14 Local authorities should have the right of recourse to a judicial remedy in order to secure free exercise of their powers and respect for the principles of local government.

Legislative powers

Local authorities should have sufficient legislative powers to give meaning to devolution, in their governmental role. This requirement can be given expression in the allocation of powers to set by-laws, which should be fully recognised by central government and by Parliament.

15 The legislative role of local authorities, expressed and supported by their powers to set by-laws, is a necessary element of their governmental role.

Other articles might be considered suitable for inclusion in the code. There is a case for including a 'right to consultation', at an appropriately early stage in the planning and decision-making processes of central government, for all matters in which local government has a direct concern. There is a case for including an article that deals with the conditions of service of local-government employees, ensuring the recruitment of high-quality staff on the basis of merit and competence. The right of councillors to an appropriate level of remuneration for the roles and responsibilities they carry out might also merit inclusion. The list of 15 principles set out and discussed above is not intended to be comprehensive. But it does cover all the key elements that should be incorporated in the code.

No doubt many of these elements could and would be challenged by the central government of the day. They would defend the need to control the overall level of local-government expenditure, arguing that it was necessary to do so to ensure that the centre's macroeconomic targets could be met (see Chapter 6 for a refutation of this argument). And they would undoubtedly challenge the limits to central intervention in the performance of local services, which is included in our proposals for the statutory code. They would do so using the now-familiar concept of the 'post-code lottery'.

Even if the principles of subsidiarity were to be agreed by central government (an unlikely, but highly desirable, outcome), they would no doubt argue that subsidiarity would need to be balanced by a recognition of the unacceptability of the post-code lottery. Using familiar health examples, such as the variations in the time that patients in hospital Accident and Emergency (A&E) departments have to wait to be treated, the argument could be extended, and indeed has been, to a range of local-government services. How can it be right that class sizes in one London Borough are significantly greater than in another? Why should residents in one metropolitan district have to make do with having their bins emptied once a fortnight when in an adjacent borough they are emptied weekly? And why should it take on average a week longer to process a planning application in one shire district compared with another? The 'postcode-lottery' argument is that across a number of services (it is not at all clear which), the public should expect the same or similar standards and outcomes, regardless of where they live, whether class sizes, for example, General Certificate of Secondary Education (GCSE) pass rates, frequencies of refuse collection, speed of response to planning applications, or incidence of child-abuse cases.

There is a superficial plausibility about the postcode-lottery argument, but it is fraught with difficulties, both of justification and implementation. There is an important distinction to be made between input and output criteria, and the way in which performance in each category should be interpreted. Variations in input criteria, such as class size, frequency of bin collection, and opening hours of libraries, should not be confused with variations in output, such as GCSE results, rates of recycling achieved, and level of use of different library services. If there is a legitimate central-government concern with local performance, it should be over output rather than input measures. Would it matter if a local authority had above-average class sizes, if it achieved well above-average GCSE results? The commitment to weekly bin collections by Eric Pickles in 2012, if implemented and replicated across the full range of council services, would indeed have turned local authorities into mere 'agents of the centre'.

The services most typically cited by the centre as justifying intervention because of unacceptable 'postcode-lottery' reasons have been education and health. Consider some examples. One local authority might decide to invest heavily in pre-school education, arguing (not unreasonably) that such investment would be likely to reap dividends in educational achievements (which can be measured) and social skills (which would be more difficult to assess). As a result of this longer-term strategy, its investment in secondary education is reduced, and its A-level results remain (for a time) below average. Is there a case here for central intervention?

Our argument would be that there is not. The local authority is making a legitimate and reasonable local choice, which the party in power may have included in its election manifesto, before implementing it. It is doing what local authorities are supposed to do – that is, exercising local choice. Another local authority might decide to make a different choice about investment at different stages in the education process, which would (or should) be equally acceptable. Similarly, one council might take a long time in coming to decisions about local planning applications, because it wished to ensure that the decisions it made were robust and evidence based, taking into account all relevant considerations and local views, but as a consequence take longer to process them.

While health authorities are not at present elected authorities (although health budgets are currently being devolved to one or two of the Combined Authorities; see Chapter 9), the same principles of local choice are relevant. One such choice, when health authorities had (as they did until recently) the responsibility for public health, would have been to invest heavily in that function, in the expectation that by doing so, they would reduce the need for acute hospital services in the locality in the future. But the level of investment they decided might mean that other local health services were less well-resourced than in neighbouring authorities, and as a result waiting times at A&E departments were higher than average, and hence a possible cause for concern on 'postcode-lottery' grounds. As with the education example above, this choice would seem to be legitimate and reasonable, focusing on long-term rather than short-term outcomes.

There are implications for postcode-lottery arguments between services, as well as within them, as in the education example. Local government is about setting priorities, always within budgetary constraints. Thus, in one case a council may wish to invest heavily in safeguarding the local environment, to provide a sustainable environment for future generations. As a result, there is less cash available for other services, whose performance measures may be viewed as unsatisfactory in comparison with other authorities' services. But, again, it could be argued that the local authority is making a legitimate, democratically-approved local choice.

Our conclusion is that differences in the performance outcomes of local authorities should not be criticised in the negative language of a 'post-code lottery', but rather as the expression of local choice by democratically elected organisations. If all local authorities provided services to the same standards, and in the same way, there would be no point in having elected local authorities; non-elected QUANGOS would be all that would be needed to perform this role of a delivery-agency of centrally specified services. Local authorities are constituted for the government of difference; they respond to local economic, environmental, and social conditions. The unique characteristics and histories of their areas, all of which vary from one authority to another, lead to differences in the choices they make. There will be further variations in their choices, reflecting (as in central government) the different philosophies and priorities of the political parties that gain control of the council. Out of this diversity in the different choices made, there arise initiatives and innovations, from which others can and do learn. The implication of seeking to counteract the misconceived 'problem' of the post-code lottery would be the inhibition of initiative and innovation. The management of uniformity does not encourage such qualities.

In our discussion of the content of a statutory code to regulate central–local government relations, we suggested that one of the principles (No 11) should be to limit intervention by the centre to where there was clear evidence of serious performance failure (as in the breakdown of child safeguarding in Rotherham), based on mutually agreed criteria of what constituted 'performance failure'. Another example might be where educational achievement (as measured by A/S level results) was well below average in a local authority, even when allowance was made for the socio-economic profile of its students, and this underperformance persisted. In these circumstances it would be appropriate for the Office for Standards in Education, Children's Services and Skills (OFSTED) to be brought in. The key criteria for central intervention should be 'it doesn't matter if it's different; it does matter if there's clear evidence of serious performance failure'. Intervention by exception should be the principle adopted, rather than an unnecessary and ultimately unachievable attempt to eliminate, or minimise, post-code-lottery differences across a range of services.

The 15 principles set out earlier in this chapter in the proposed statutory code, including the key concept of subsidiarity, together with the emphasis on local choice in the discussion on the post-code lottery, provide guidelines for deciding how service and functional responsibilities should be allocated between central and local government. The onus should be on central government to justify why a service that affects local people should not be the responsibility of local government. In addition, if the centre wished to impose directions on the content of a service that is the responsibility of local government, it should also set out a reasoned justification for doing so. The arguments should be heard and decided by the proposed Joint Committee of both Houses of Parliament. If the government were successful, in its views, the proposal should be then taken forward through primary legislation, eliminating government by secondary legislation, which has become the norm as the basis for central intervention, encouraging the involvement of government departments not merely in the detail of what local authorities should do, but how also how they should do it.

It is outside the scope of this book to set out detailed proposals on a service-by-service basis about how responsibilities should be allocated between centre and locality. The important points to stress, as we have done in this chapter, are the principles on which this allocation should be made, and the processes that should be involved. It may, nonetheless, be helpful to evaluate some of the centre's recent initiatives from our localist perspective, as set out above.

Education

When discussing the 2012 Localism Act in Chapter 3, we drew attention to the fact that central-government departments other than the DCLG had virtually ignored the implications of the government's localism agenda for the services for which they were responsible. Nowhere was this neglect more apparent than in the Department for Education, where Michael Gove's priority was to stimulate the transfer of as many local-authority schools to academy status and the establishment of as many 'free schools' as possible (both of which are directly financed by central government and operate independently of the local authorities in which they are located). This measure was a flagrant example of centralisation rather than localisation. It was as if Michael Gove had never heard of the localism agenda, or perhaps more likely he had chosen to ignore it. There has been no subsequent evidence that academies (or free schools) have performed any better than those still operating within the ambit of local authorities. Yet the Conservative government elected in 2015 was minded to include in its first Queen's Speech a proposal to transform all schools remaining with local authorities into academies. The proposal was withdrawn, following widespread protests from Conservative- (and Labour-) controlled authorities with education responsibilities. Had it been enacted, it would have virtually eliminated the role of local education authorities, on the basis of an ideological predisposition shared by successive secretaries of state for education, and indeed by David Cameron himself. It is to combat this kind of unjustified central-government intervention that a statutory code regulating central–local relations urgently needs to be introduced.

The future role of local authorities in education is one of the most important challenges to be faced. The drift to centralisation, apparent since the 1980s, has over the past few years become a surge. Yet, the rationale behind the recent changes has not received the critical analysis in the media it merits. It is a priority in any attempt to rebuild local government as a viable counterbalance to the dominance of the centre that the current imbalance between centre and locality should be reappraised, not least because of the limited capacity of the centre to understand the diverse reality of local circumstances.

Policing and crime prevention

Given that much of the work of local police forces interconnects in various ways with the responsibilities of local authorities, it seems inconsistent that accountability for police matters should be channelled through a single individual who (the Mayor and Greater London Authority excepted) operates in isolation from the local authority or authorities in their localities. Elected police commissioners, introduced in 2012 to widespread public apathy in the polls, are a further example (as are directly elected mayors) of the belief of successive governments since 1997 in the benefits of individual leadership, preferably involving leaders with what are believed to be charismatic traits. In reality, the benefits of this individualised form of leadership are unproven and contestable, particularly when it is detached from the mainstream of local democratic policy-making and co-ordinated action. In the Combined Authorities that have agreed to the introduction of elected mayors, the role of mayor will be combined with that of police commissioner, which is a step in the right direction. But our preference would be for the restoration of the pre-2012 Police Committees, where there was the opportunity for more wide-ranging public debate, as well as a greater level of shared responsibility for policing and clearer democratic accountability.

Social housing

The provision of social housing is a local service, where the level and composition of need varies significantly from local authority to authority, but where demand exceeds supply in all authorities. In the spirit of the subsidiarity principle, there is no reason why local authorities should not be permitted to build social housing, and let it at affordable rates. In so doing they would be making a substantial contribution to alleviating the ever-growing housing crisis experienced by those on lower incomes, as they did so successfully in the 25 years after the end of World War II.

Health

The National Health Service (NHS) has for so long been part of the country's public-sector landscape in its own right as a single albeit decentralised entity that it might appear heretical to advocate a localist alternative. Yet, there are powerful arguments for moving in that direction. There are its links with public health (since 2013 a local-government responsibility) and with social services, particularly care for the elderly, the mentally ill, and the mentally handicapped. Health services, including many hospitals, used to be provided by local authorities. In the 1945–1950 Labour government Herbert Morrison wanted this responsibility to remain with local authorities when the NHS was established, but he lost out in cabinet to Nye Bevan, who later acknowledged that the lack of democratic control in the NHS was a 'key mistake'. It is common in other European countries for health services to be a local-government responsibility. Applying the principles of subsidiarity, local choice, democratic accountability, and the need for the strategic co-ordination of interrelated local services, there is a strong case for most health services to be transferred to local authorities. Indeed, that is exactly what has happened recently, when the health budget for Greater Manchester was transferred from the NHS to the Greater Manchester Combined Authority, a process which may be extended to other such areas. Perhaps the bringing of the NHS under local democratic control can no longer be regarded as heresy!

Competitive tendering

Finally, there is the issue of the legitimacy of the centre requiring local authorities to put a range of services out to competitive tender (with the expectation that the contract should go to the lowest bidder). This approach was introduced, and then extended, by the Thatcher-led Conservative governments from 1983 onwards, one of the earliest examples of the intrusion of central government into how local authorities operate, as opposed to what they do. There were worrying signs in the *Open Public Services White Paper* of 2011 (Cm. 8145) (CLG 2011b) that the government intended to introduce new requirements on local authorities to extend competitive tendering. We see no justification for central-government interference in such matters. If local authorities wish to outsource particular services, that's not a problem. But, equally, if they prefer to deliver services 'in house', which has the advantage of providing flexibility to modify service provision in response to unforeseen changes in circumstances without the need to renegotiate contracts, then that should be just as acceptable. Such matters are better left subject to local choice.

6

RETHINKING LOCAL-GOVERNMENT FINANCE

The constitutional changes proposed in the previous chapter will have little impact unless they are supported by a system of local-government finance that permits local authorities to implement them fully. A general power of competence is of little current value to authorities who are struggling to make decisions on which services to cut. In this chapter, we develop arguments as to why the present level of central control over local-government finance is both unnecessary and unhelpful. Different options for financing local government are then explored and comparatively evaluated, and some key principles set out. Finally, the proposals of the Conservative government on local government (several of which originated from the previous Chancellor of the Exchequer, George Osborne) are critically analysed. This chapter does not attempt a comprehensive review of local-government finance. Some of the more detailed measures currently in operation, such as specific grants, growth funds, local economic partnerships, the Better Care Fund, and the various bidding mechanisms, important though they are, are less germane to the broader issues on which this book focuses.

The case against central control

There are two reasons for rethinking the system of local-government finance. The first, as we emphasised earlier, is that the current system is a mess and unsustainable in any move towards a regeneration of local government based on the principles set out in the previous chapter, which we put forward to stimulate a reversal of the dangerous drift towards an increasingly centralised and ineffective state. The problems with the current financial arrangements stem from their incoherent nature, and in particular from the inappropriate imbalance between the proportion of local-government expenditure that is centrally financed (much too high) and the proportion that is raised locally (much too low). This mismatch greatly limits the scope for changes in the levels of council tax, since to finance a 1 per cent increase in expenditure requires, on average, a 2 per cent increase in council tax (until the recent introduction of a 100 per cent schools grant, a 4 per cent increase in council tax was required to finance a 1 per cent increase in expenditure). In addition, restrictions imposed by the centre on the permissible level of council-tax increases (in all authorities) have resulted, in effect, in expenditure-capping.

The second is a more positive reason than escaping from the errors of the past. This book sets out a vision of what the role and nature of local government should be, if we are to overcome the ever-increasing centralisation of our system of government. This vision involves the genuine devolution of powers to local authorities, based on the principle of subsidiarity, which would give local authorities a responsibility for the well-being of their local communities, including but extending beyond their role in the provision of services. These reforms would create authorities capable of responding to the variety of needs that face them rather than imposing uniformity. The system of local government finance should express and support the purpose of local government that we seek, which requires a wide-ranging scope for local choice built on the foundations of local democracy and local accountability. Such an outcome is not achieved, nor is it achievable, within the present system of local-government finance. The dependence of local authorities on government grant and capping limits the scope for choice, while the complex and largely incomprehensible system of local-government finance makes genuine accountability impossible, since it limits public understanding of where responsibility for local public action really lies. The system turns local authorities into bodies lobbying central government for more resources, or, in more recent times, pressing government to limit the level of cuts in their allocation of resources. The kind of local authorities we would like to see should take full responsibility for the choices they make, taking account of their impact upon local expenditure levels, and hence local taxation, which would provide a much more transparent basis for local accountability than the present confusing system.

Since the early 1980s successive governments have imposed restrictions on the permitted levels of revenue expenditure of individual local authorities, or on permitted levels of increase in council tax (formerly on rates increases) or both. At first, such controls were introduced selectively, but for the past ten years all local authorities have been subjected to such restrictions.

Can the current central-government controls over local-government finance be justified? The familiar argument is that it is necessary in the economic interests of the country for central government to set what is an acceptable future level for total managed expenditure (TME), within which all local-government expenditure is included. Central government asserts that it has to control the overall level of expenditure by all local authorities because it does not trust local government to comply voluntarily; hence, universal 'council-tax capping' is an essential element of the system.

The case in principle for the government seeking to control public expenditure is uncontentious. But the case for including all local-government expenditure in the calculation is not. The grant that central government distributes annually to local authorities should be included, not the total level of local-government expenditure. Revenues raised locally to finance local-government expenditure, including local taxation and other revenue raised locally, do not affect TME, since local authorities do not have powers to borrow to cover their revenue expenditure, unlike central government and, it would appear, health authorities.

Local-authority revenue expenditure should not therefore form part of a macro-economic forecasting and targeting system. Indeed, its inclusion undermines what was, until the 1980s, a well-established principle that it was the right of each local authority to set its local tax at a level that enabled it to meet its perceived expenditure needs. That principle should be re-introduced as part of a new constitutional settlement.

What is also required is a form of central–local financial settlement that provides more flexibility in local budgeting than the current system allows. If local authorities were able to raise about two-thirds of their income locally, then their scope for genuine local choice would be greatly enhanced. But central-government grant should remain as a key element in local-government finance, to compensate for the disparities in both the intensity of needs and the availability of resources among different local authorities. Compare, for example, the socio-economic differences and the disparity in scope for raising resources locally between Surrey County Council and Stoke-on-Trent City Council, or between the London Boroughs of Westminster and Waltham Forest. Hence, a two-thirds to one-third average ratio of local sources of funding to funding provided by central government would need to be operated with a degree of flexibility. Central-funding allocations to different authorities would need to be responsive to these differences in local needs and resources, as was the case until the 1980s, although it should be borne in mind that the involvement of central government in the equalisation process (and in the assessment of needs) is itself a contributory element to centralisation.

What are the options?

Four main methods of local taxation have dominated discussions about local-government finance since the most recent authoritative independent review of the subject, carried out by the Layfield Committee, which reported in 1976. They are as follows:

- local residential property tax;
- local tax on non-residential properties;
- local income tax;
- local per capita tax.

There are other possibilities, which are listed and briefly discussed later in this chapter. But these four form the basis of the subsequent discussion.

Until 1990 domestic and non-domestic rates together constituted the main sources of local finance (the levying of fees and charges was a further, relatively minor, source). At this time non-domestic rates were a genuine local source of finance, because they were set and collected locally. There was then a brief and controversial interlude from 1990 (1989 in Scotland) to 1993, when domestic rates were replaced by a local per capita tax, officially designated as the community charge, but widely known as the poll tax. Non-domestic rates continued, but ceased to operate as a local tax, in that they were now set and collected nationally, and then redistributed to local authorities, in effect as a further element of central-government grant. In 1993, the community charge was replaced by council tax, which was to a large extent a residential property tax, but contained an element of per capita tax relief, since discounts are available for single householders, those under 18, and full-time students. Before 1990 expenditure financed from local sources accounted for 53 per cent of total local-government expenditure. After 1992 the figure dropped to 15 per cent, and has increased only marginally since. This imbalance is at the root of local authorities' financial problems and lack of scope for real choice. Local income tax was recommended by the Layfield Committee (see Chapter 2) as a supplement to the retention of a domestic rates-based system, and has been reintroduced to the agenda at various times since, but has never been adopted by central government.

What are the criteria that should be used to compare and evaluate the appropriateness of the four methods of local taxation outlined above? The 1981 Green Paper on Local Government Finance provided a comprehensive list:

- Practicability: has it the capacity to produce a substantial yield?
- Comprehensibility: is it easy to understand?
- Fairness: does it relate to people's ability to pay?
- Acceptability: would it command broad public support?
- Accountability: would it be paid directly by most people who benefit from the services provided?
- Cost-effectiveness: could administrative and collection costs be kept within reasonable limits?

The other criteria listed included efficiency, perceptibility, predictability, buoyancy, and suitability (for different tiers), but the six we have singled out have formed the main reference points in comparative evaluation of different approaches.

The community charge, or poll tax, is widely regarded as a prime example of a policy disaster. It did have its strengths – for example, practicability, comprehensibility, and accountability. Its weaknesses included (perceived) unfairness, unacceptability, and cost-ineffectiveness. Whatever the case in principle for its reintroduction, it is inconceivable in the light of its recent history that any government would propose to do so. Hence we do not discuss it further here. The same point might be made about local income tax, despite the strong (in principle) case that can be made for it (it is comprehensible, fair, accountable, and cost effective). It would also have the advantage of being more equitable, in that all local taxpayers would contribute to the financing of local services rather than just heads of households. In this respect it would achieve a similar (and laudable) aim of the community charge, that of widening the scope of local accountability (in that far more voters would have to consider the financial consequences of casting their votes at local elections, but would so with a much stronger emphasis on 'ability to pay'). Unfortunately, it has been perceived by previous governments as unacceptable in the eyes of the public, who, it is claimed, would be strongly opposed to paying an additional tranche of income tax (despite the widespread adoption of this measure in many other countries, including Scotland and, in the next few years, Wales). But, in principle, the level of local income tax charged should be balanced by a proportionate reduction in the level of national income tax, to allow for the fact that central government would no longer be responsible for the local expenditure covered by the local income tax, and hence could reduce national taxation levels proportionately. Although we see a strong case for the Layfield Commission's recommendation that local income tax should be used as a supplement to a local domestic property tax, we also recognise political realities that make its introduction unlikely in the short term.

The two remaining options, local taxes on residential and non-residential properties, respectively, feature prominently in the government's current plans for radical change in local finance, which are discussed later in this chapter. There is no inclination at present to discontinue some form of local property tax, for good reasons. It has the merits of comprehensibility, fairness (particularly when operated in conjunction with a range of discounts), cost-effectiveness, and (for domestic properties at least) accountability. Its fairness has been questioned (the familiar example of the little old lady living alone in a large house), but such concerns can be mitigated by the adoption of a range of discounts linked to ability to pay as, to some extent, happened with the community charge. Its level of accountability has come under scrutiny, since only the head of the household receives the bill rather than each adult member of the household. But other adult members of a household have the right to express their concerns with the level of the tax at local elections, and in this sense there is a transparent accountability link. Layfield saw no reason not to recommend the continuation of a domestic property tax (at that time, the rates) and, with one notable and disastrous exception, no subsequent government has taken a contrary view.

But the appropriateness of the use of non-domestic rates as a source of local finance is more questionable. There are potential attractions. If it were to operate as a genuinely local tax – that is, one that was set and collected by each individual local authority – then it would contribute to a substantial reduction in the level of dependence of local authorities on central grant. It could also be argued that it would focus the attention of authorities on incentives for business growth in their areas. It meets the criteria of practicability and cost-effectiveness. And there is also an 'in principle' case that as local businesses benefit in various ways from the services provided by local authorities – roads, public transport, waste collection, the education of the local workforce – it is only fair that they should contribute to the local council's finances.

But there are two major problems associated with business rates as a local tax. The first is that the amount of resources they raised would vary considerably from authority to authority, because of variations in the prevalence of industrial and commercial concerns in different areas (compare, for example, the resources that would be raised by the business rate in the City of Westminster, compared with a largely residential outer borough such as Harrow or Sutton). This disparity would create a prima facie case for redistribution. But if redistribution were to become part of the system, which is the proposal that currently appears to be favoured in the Local Government Association's attempts to reach agreement on the form of the business rate to be adopted, then the business rate would cease to qualify as a local tax, and would revert to its current status as a constituent of central grant. It would, however, be possible to deliver such 'within area' redistribution by giving the upper tier (Greater London Authority, or GLA, and counties) a larger share of the revenue. If the GLA held most or all of business rates, then the Westminster/Sutton disparities would matter less.

The second major problem is that the degree of variation in the level of business rates set (in the absence of redistribution) would increase the complexity of the system with its tangle of tariffs and top-ups, and, as a result, increase the difficulty of the public and businesses in understanding the impact of the tax. It would lack comprehensibility. This lack of clarity, in turn, causes problems of accountability, which is the tax's most serious defect. It is not clear how mechanisms of accountability are supposed to operate. Is accountability focused on the customers of the business, who may not be citizens of the local authority in which the business is located, and will include people from well outside the area? Or is it focused on owners and shareholders, who may also live outside the area of the authority? There is certainly no guarantee in either case that the constituency involved will be made up wholly or even mainly of local electors. Accountability is further weakened by the fact that businesses per se are not entitled to vote in local elections, nor is it feasible or desirable that they should. For all these reasons there is a strong case for arguing that the business rate is more appropriately viewed as a national rather than a local tax.

The lack of clear accountability is the main reason for resisting the use of business rates as a key component of the local dimension of a new system of local finance, although we can understand the appeal of its reintroduction for local authorities in the current climate of austerity, not least because it is all that is presently on offer.

In seeking clarity of accountability there is much to be said for the introduction of local income tax, as a supplement to a local property tax, as Layfield recommended. This option may well be considered politically unacceptable by the centre, and even by many in local government. But if that is the right course, the LGA should argue strongly for it and not concede prematurely.

However, there are other ways in which the current council tax could be strengthened as the major local source of local government finance. The most important way in which the local tax base could be strengthened is through a revaluation of residential property, accompanied by the introduction of a wider range of council-tax bands. The valuation that underpinned the introduction of council tax took place in 1991, nearly 25 years ago. A revaluation is long overdue, and there is a precedent in the nationwide revaluation of commercial property that will shortly be completed. Wales, uniquely, revalued its council tax in 2005 and added an additional value band. The introduction of a much wider range of council-tax bands would generate a substantial increase in council income. There would be no need for a separate 'mansion tax', if this change were to be introduced. Although all parts of the country would benefit, it would be a particularly fruitful source of council-tax income in Greater London, where the tax imposed on the residents of luxury mansions and expensive town houses would be made to reflect more closely their current value, whereas at present the top property-value band covers a wide range of properties, most of which have a value well below the highest levels. This move would increase the fairness of the council tax, particularly from the perspective of those who could never aspire to the ownership of a luxury mansion.

The financial benefit to authorities with higher property values, such as many London boroughs, could be counterbalanced by a reduction in central-government grant, reflecting their lack of need for a 'resources' element of grant. It is not unlikely that some London boroughs would end up in a position where they could operate independently of central grant, which was one of George Osborne's aims in his November 2015 spending review. But this outcome could not be expected in the much-less-affluent cities of the north of England.

To strengthen the fairness of this reconstructed form of council tax, it would be essential to continue to apply the discounts currently in operation, and ideally to widen the scope of dispensations, to lessen the impact upon low-income households. If, as would be likely, council tax came to be a significantly higher proportion of the financial resources of most councils, then it would be important to incorporate into the change some form of transitional arrangement to avoid an outcome whereby households in the lower- and middle-income ranges experienced a substantial net increase in their local tax payments between one year and the next, which was one of the many problems associated with the introduction of the community charge. Or it might be easier to specify that new, higher bills should take effect only when a transaction takes place at the point of sale. But this matter of detail could and should be equitably dealt with, and it does not detract from the importance of moving to a system of local-government finance dependent more on local revenue sources than central ones.

In several European countries (see below) local authorities are permitted to exploit more than one source of local revenue. Combinations of property tax, local income tax, local sales tax, and tourism tax are all possibilities. It is beyond the scope of this book to provide a detailed comparison of their relative strengths and weaknesses, which were laid out in the Layfield Committee's report, but we would recommend that such an exercise should be conducted by an independent body before a new system of local government finance is introduced. It should also be possible, as in several European countries, for local authorities to be able to choose amongst different types of local tax. However, in the shorter term the retention and modification of the current council-tax system would help facilitate the transition from the existing failing regime of local-government finance to the new, without major disruption.

The adoption of a more radical reform of the local-government finance system conferring on councils a wider range of tax-raising (and spending) powers, which could not be limited or altered by central government, would be a further important step in the direction of a substantial reduction in central control. Councils could secure their financial freedom by generating tax income from a range of property taxes as suggested by the report of the London Finance Commission of 2013, *Raising the Capital*, which recommended for London 'the full suite of property taxes, council tax, stamp duty land tax, annual tax on enveloped buildings and capital gains property disposal tax' (2013, p9 and pp63–69).

Other taxation mechanisms could be deployed. Below are some examples of the types of tax regimes that exist for local government beyond this country (see Copus, Sweeting and Wingfield 2013):

- local income tax (Belgium, Denmark, Finland, Sweden, Italy, Spain, Switzerland), as discussed in detail in the Lyons *Inquiry Report* (2009);
- general tax-raising powers (for example, dog tax, passport issuing, sewage tax, revenue from sale of brown-field land for development: Flanders and/or Holland);
- sales tax (various US states, Brazil);
- tax on the self-employed (Germany);
- entertainment tax (Croatia);
- tax on land (Denmark);
- corporate income tax (Germany, Denmark, Spain, Hungary);
- tax on patents (transferred to councils in Bulgaria);
- real-estate tax (Poland, Brazil);
- poll tax (Slovenia);
- tourist tax (Hungary);
- car tax (Spain, Croatia);
- inheritance and gift tax (Croatia).

Some of these options may not be appropriate for the UK, and that would certainly be true of a poll tax, but others are worthy of serious consideration, in particular local income tax, sales tax and a tourist tax. While the introduction of any of these taxation methods does not guarantee local-government freedom from the centre, adopting some of them would help to provide a more stable financial basis than exists at present. Alongside these taxes, the right to raise funds through commercial profit and the markets, unregulated by government and without the need for government approvals, would enhance local government's discretion and diminish the scope for central-government intervention.

The way forward

This book does not seek to provide a blueprint for reform. Set out at the end of the chapter are a number of key principles that should be included in the code governing central–local relations, which was proposed in the previous chapter. However, on the basis of the analysis carried out in this chapter, it may be helpful to highlight some of the more specific financial mechanisms that, in our view, would help to strengthen local government and free it up to play a meaningful community-governance role, which are set out below:

- In the short term, there should be three main constituents of local government finance: council tax, scope to raise a local income tax (as in Scotland and (soon) in Wales), and central-government grant to provide an equalisation mechanism to respond to disparities in the revenue-raising capacity of different authorities.

- Central-government equalisation responsibilities should be limited in scope to avoid the dangers of handing power back to the centralisers. They should concentrate on disparities in resources, rather than disparities in needs. Measures could include sub-national equalising pools at the city- or county-regional level or intervention by the centre to build up the economic performance of seriously lagging authorities.

- It is inappropriate to regard non-domestic (or business) rates as a legitimate source of locally generated finance, because of the problems of local accountability associated with them. They should be retained in full by local authorities, but in the form of a component of central grant, distributed in a way that gives upper-tier authorities a larger share of the revenue.

- A revaluation of domestic property should take place, to provide a fairer basis for council tax. It should incorporate the introduction of a wider range of council-tax bands, to deal in particular with the wide range of property values in the current highest band.

The government's plans

George Osborne's November 2015 Spending Review included a series of proposed adjustments to the system of local-government finance, some of them far-reaching in their consequences. One of his most significant aims was to reduce drastically the reliance of all local authorities on central-government grant by the year 2020. In principle, this objective is desirable if it assists in facilitating the scope for local choice and the strengthening of local accountability. However, one of the key mechanisms for achieving this goal is the restoration to local authorities of business rates, which we have argued has serious problems as a local tax. In addition, the lack of any reference to how the government intends to deal with the substantial disparities in needs and resources among different authorities, and the importance of including some form of compensatory mechanism that recognises these differences are worrying omissions. There is also no indication that the current capping mechanisms on the level of permitted council-tax increases are to be removed.

The Spending Review included provision for a 56 per cent reduction in central-government grant in the period up to 2020, involving a reduction from UK£11.5 billion per year to £5.4 billion. However, it was argued by the Department for Communities and Local Government (DCLG) that if one took into account grants, council tax, business rates, and other funding pots, the 'headline figure' was a 6.7 per cent reduction over the five-year period. The chancellor himself claimed that local government would 'spend the same in cash terms as it does today' in 2020, a claim that was quickly challenged by Chartered Institute of Public Finance and Accountancy (CIPFA) chief executive Rob Whiteman, who expressed the view that this claim includes 'some deft and dodgy arithmetic on devolution' (Municipal Journal 26 November 2015, p1).

The chancellor reiterated his plan to return business rates to local authorities, but specified that only elected mayors of combined authorities would have the power to raise them, a move that is difficult to justify, other than as a bribe to gain local support for directly elected mayors. There was some relaxation in the permitted scope for increases in council tax, which in previous years had been limited to 2 per cent (although a local authority could put forward a proposal for a greater increase in a local referendum, but none had done so). His proposal was that councils with social-care responsibilities would be permitted to levy an additional rise in council tax of 2 per cent, provided that the funds raised were spent exclusively on adult social care. He went on to claim that as much as £2 billion could be raised by 2020, if all councils imposed a 2 per cent precept.

This package constituted a strange mixture of enhanced sources of local funding, through the transfer of business rates: a marginal freeing-up of council tax-capping restrictions, and what was in effect a limited specific grant earmarked for social care, which could not be spent on an authority's own priorities. Osborne's stated intention was to shift substantially the balance of funding from central grant to local sources of income by 2020, which lacks credibility when one recognises that the business rate will continue to operate as a de facto central grant. The devil, as so often, is in the detail, and the response of the local government world (as represented by the LGA) to the package was far from positive. The then LGA chairman, the Conservative Lord Porter, claimed that 'even if councils stopped filling in potholes, closed all children's centres, libraries, museums, leisure centres and turned off every street light, they will not have saved enough money to plug the financial black hole they face by 2020' (Municipal Journal 26 November 2015, p1).

Once there had been the chance to examine Osborne's package of proposals in more detail, and reflect on their impact upon different local authorities, it became clear that they would affect different authorities in various ways, an issue to which little serious thought appeared to have been given. The disparity between the better-off and more deprived local authorities will influence the extent to which they will benefit from the proposals to localise business rates, and from the permitted 2 per cent precept in council tax earmarked for social care. It will also influence the extent to which they will gain or lose from the proposed switch (scheduled to take place between 2015 and 2020) from central grant to council tax and non-domestic rates as a source of local-government funding.

Similarly, assuming restrictions continue to be placed for the duration of this parliament on the percentage rise in council tax that councils will be permitted to set (unless they seek authority to set a higher increase through a referendum), then such restrictions will continue to have more serious consequences for some authorities than for others. In authorities where house prices are high (Kensington and Chelsea again, plus a whole range of other affluent London boroughs), the per capita yield of a 1 per cent increase in council tax is, other things being equal, considerably higher than in more deprived areas in the provinces (such as Liverpool, Barrow, Sunderland, and Walsall), where the pressure on resources stemming from high deprivation is much greater.

There is a similar problem about the potential benefits of the opportunity to raise council tax by 2 per cent to fund the increased demand for adult social care. A detailed critique of this proposal from the influential think tank the Kings Fund (2015) concluded that places in the North, the Midlands, and the poorer boroughs of inner London will lose out because they will be able to raise too little revenue from it to make any real difference. The measure will, they claim, 'widen the gap between richer and poorer areas, and raise only UK£800 million a year – far less than the £2 billion predicted'.

The Kings Fund prediction of the level of the shortfall turned out to be a significant underestimate. A survey by the Association of Adult Social Services Directors (which received a 100 per cent return) that the 2 per cent social-care precept raised only £380 million, rather than the £2 billion estimated by the government when it announced the policy. As predicted by the Kings Fund, the precept raised least in the areas of greatest need. In addition, the extra funding of £380 million that has been realised has been more than swallowed up by the costs of implementing the national living-wage. As a consequence, local authorities were forced in 2016–2017 to make further cuts in their social care budgets of nearly UK£1 billion, on top of the £5 billion made since 2010.

What this outcome illustrates is the futility of such ad hoc piecemeal financial initiatives introduced by the centre, particularly where they neglect the considerable differences in the revenue-raising potential of a specified percentage increase in council tax in different authorities. A lifting of all restrictions on council-tax increases and local-authority expenditure decision-making would be a more effective way of enabling local authorities to manage their resources, so that they could respond to challenges like the ever-increasing demand for adult social-care services, generated by the changing age profile of the country. Even this essential measure would need to be accompanied, as we argued earlier in this chapter, by a switch in the balance of central–local funding of council expenditure in favour of the latter, supported by a system of allocation of the (reduced) central grant that makes proper allowance for disparities in both the needs faced and resource-generation potential of different local authorities.

Meanwhile, the LGA, having been given the responsibility for proposing guidelines as to how the resources generated by the full retention of business rates by local government should be distributed amongst local authorities, has struggled to reach agreement. Predictably, the main sticking point was what the London boroughs should receive in the redistribution formula. London councils announced in June 2016 that they were exploring the option of keeping every penny of the approximately UK£6.6 billion it collects in business rates, a decision that understandably angered other LGA territorial groupings. The finance spokesman for the County Councils Network, David Barrow, said he was shocked to hear that London was still pushing proposals that were 'so at odds with the rest of local government', adding that 'it is totally preposterous that 20 per cent of the population should get 40 per cent of the country's business rates' (Municipal Journal 16 June 2016, p1).

In June 2016 the referendum vote to leave the EU was quickly followed by the resignation of David Cameron, the selection of Theresa May as prime minister, and George Osborne's term as Chancellor of the Exchequer coming to an end. His replacement, Philip Hammond, has done little to suggest a change in financial policy towards local government. The emphasis on austerity and further cuts in expenditure look set to continue on the basis of his 2016 Autumn Statement. Whatever further changes he may introduce, the analysis and arguments set out in this chapter remain relevant key aspects in any consideration of a move to a system of local-government finance that would enhance local government autonomy and accountability. The same is true of the key principles set out below.

Key principles of local-government finance

In the previous chapter, which considered the case for constitutional change and outlined key principles that should be included in a statutory code, we proposed a principle for dealing with local-government finance, which stated, 'Local authorities should be entitled to adequate financial resources of their own, of which they may dispose freely within the framework of their statutory powers.' This chapter has set out to apply this principle to the current package of proposals involving the funding of local government, and has found them inconsistent with this principle. Listed below are a further set of principles, to underpin the way in which the financing of local government should be organised, and included in the code:

- Local authorities' financial resources shall be commensurate with their responsibilities.
- All the financial resources of local authorities shall derive from local taxes and charges, over which they will have the power to determine the rate. The only exceptions should be grants to correct the effects of the unequal distribution of potential sources of finance and the financial burdens they must bear.
- Capping of local-government revenue expenditure in any of its forms by central government undermines the principles of local government.
- The financial systems on which resources available to local authorities are based should be of a sufficiently diversified and buoyant nature to enable them to keep pace with the cost of carrying out their tasks.
- All capping of local-government expenditure, whether directly or indirectly (through an imposed referendum), should be discontinued.
- For the purpose of borrowing for capital investment, local authorities should have access to the national capital market.
- The local-government financial system should express and support local choice and local accountability for which local authorities should be responsible to the local electorate.

7

POLITICS, PARTIES, AND LOCAL DEMOCRACY

Central intervention in the management of local authorities

In the absence of a constitution that would protect local government from arbitrary interference by the centre, central government can, whenever it wishes, change any aspect of the operations of local government including territorial structure (which it has modified at regular intervals over the past 50 years; see Chapter 8), voting systems (which it changed in Scotland from first past the post to a form of PR in 2000), and political-management arrangements.

However, only relatively recently has central government felt it necessary to intervene in the political-management arrangements of local authorities. Up until the 1980s it was largely left to local authorities to decide how they:

- organised their decision-making structures (including numbers and designations of committees, and sub-committees), with only one or two exceptions, which were discontinued at the time of the 1974 reorganisation;
- organised their management arrangements (with the exception of a longstanding requirement in education authorities to appoint a chief education officer);
- ran the services for which they were responsible – for example, although there was nothing to stop a local authority contracting out the provision of a service, there was no requirement for them to do so.

The 1983–1987 and 1987–1992 Conservative governments introduced a legal requirement for local authorities to submit a range of services (including refuse collection and housing maintenance) to competitive tender, with a presumption in favour of the lowest bidder. And in the wake of the report of the Widdicombe Committee (*The Conduct of Local Authority Business*, 1986) the government brought in legislation that required authorities to identify within their management structures a 'head of paid service', a 'monitoring officer', and a Section 151 officer (to ensure financial propriety). But it was left to local authorities to decide which officers should carry out these roles. There was no legal requirement to appoint a chief executive (and there still isn't), nor a council leader (a county as large as Surrey in 1970s chose not to designate a leader). It was not until after Labour came to power in the 1997 general election that the freedom of local authorities in decision-making and management structures was curtailed, a move that brought the process of centralisation into previously unchartered territory (and, in doing so, involved more than 200 pages of secondary legislation and detailed guidance):

- In the Local Government Act 2000 the Labour government determined that the long-established committee system should be abolished in all authorities except those shire districts with a population of 85,000 or below; they could choose to retain it.
- The same act required all councils who did not introduce one of the two 'elected mayor' options to designate a leader of the council, and appoint a cabinet of not more than ten members, to exercise the executive functions previously carried out by committees.
- The act provided an opportunity for councils to operate with an elected mayor if a local referendum voted in favour of doing so (the referendum could be triggered by the council itself or by a petition signed by 5 per cent of the council's electorate).
- It introduced a requirement that all authorities should establish one or more scrutiny committees.

Later during its period of government, it introduced a requirement that all authorities with responsibility for education and social services must appoint a 'Director of Children's Services', followed later by a requirement to establish a Health Scrutiny Committee. The Local Government Act 2009 made provision for a four-year scrutiny of tenure for council leaders, dating from the time that they first acceded to this position, and also empowered them to appoint (and dismiss) cabinet members, designate (and change) their portfolios, and specify the individual decision-making powers (if any) of each cabinet colleague.

The initial set of changes set out in the 2000 Act had been reasonably well thought through. Justifications were provided for them as strengthening the visibility, accountability, and transparency of local decision-making. But it set a precedent for central government to introduce legislative requirements over how local authorities should carry out their business, in ways that involved a worrying level of detail. The case that such choices (and details) could best be left to local authorities themselves was not addressed in the formulation of the act.

However, the changes introduced in the 2009 Local Government Act cannot be argued to have been remotely 'well considered'. As noted above, in its desire to encourage strong and stable leadership, the government included in the statute the 'security of tenure' provision for non-mayoral council leaders.

This provision demonstrates a bizarre misunderstanding of the different patterns of the electoral timetable in local authorities. It appears to be based on the premise that all authorities hold elections, every four years, in which case it would be feasible (although by no means fool-proof) to introduce such a 'security of tenure' provision. But whereas London boroughs, shire counties, most unitary authorities, and about two-thirds of the shire districts operate on this basis, the remainder (about 100 in total), including big cities such as Manchester, Liverpool, and Sheffield, do not. Here, elections are held three years out of four. It is therefore possible (and, indeed, in politically changeable authorities, not unlikely) that the leaders elected in year one, (when their parties won a majority) will face in years two or three a changed political composition with the majority lost. What would be the implication of the 'security of tenure' principle for a Labour leader whose party loses control to the Conservatives a year after his accession, or for a Conservative leader losing his or her overall majority, where the Labour and Liberal Democrat parties are minded to form a coalition? The reality is they would be in an unsustainable position. By law they can insist on staying in office, but faced with a numerically superior opposition, they could not hope to get measures (including the budget) through the council?

Even in authorities that operate a four-year electoral cycle, if the leader loses the confidence of the party group, it is highly unlikely that they could continue to operate in any meaningful sense as 'council leader'? The Conservative leaders of Suffolk and Cornwall county councils both stepped down (despite their nominal 'security of tenure') in 2012–2013 because of mounting opposition within their parties over ambitious outsourcing proposals supported by the leaders.

It is not clear whether, given these inconsistencies, the government had simply failed to think through the implications of the 'security of tenure' provision, or whether it was being wilfully mischievous ('let's include it and leave local authorities to sort out what to do if there's a change of control'). Either way the measure was an ill-considered and unnecessary intervention by central government as to how local authorities should manage their own operations. It illustrates the extent to which centralisation has pervaded the detail of local matters that would be better left to local authorities themselves.

Elected mayors and the myth of the strong leader

These imposed changes in the political-management structures of local authorities have had major effects on their political culture. They have strengthened the role of the council leader. Central government has an obsession with strong leadership that is not always congruent with local political traditions, particularly in the Liberal Democrat and (some) Labour parties. The virtues of strong leadership are, in any event, highly contestable. Professor Archie Brown in his authoritative study of political leadership, *The Myth of the Strong Leader*, writes:

> The idea that the more power one individual leader wields, the more we should be impressed by that leader is an illusion … there are many qualities desirable in a political leader that should matter more than the criterion of strength … far more desirable than the model of political leader as master is collective leadership
>
> *(Brown 2014, pp1–2)*

Central government's obsession with 'strong leadership' is relatively recent in origin. It underpinned the provisions of the 2000 Local Government Act that required all local authorities with a population of 85,000 or above to adopt either an 'elected mayor' or 'cabinet and leader' model. The enthusiasm for elected mayors, as a symbol of strong leadership, continued throughout the 1997–2010 period of office of the Labour government, and looked at times as if it might be imposed (in certain circumstances) on local authorities. It is likely that it was only the indifference of John Prescott (whose responsibilities included local government from 1997 to 2005) to the idea of elected mayors that pre-empted this imposition. Labour's enthusiasm for the linked concepts of 'strong leadership' and 'elected mayors' was matched by that of the 2010–15 coalition, which in the months before the 2015 general election, insisted that Combined Authorities that wanted to enjoy the widest range of devolutionary measures on offer must be prepared to accept an elected mayor as part of the deal (see Chapter 7).

Vibrant Local Leadership (ODPM 2005) argued that 'continual improvement requires strong and effective leadership; it is about bringing other stakeholders together to help deliver this vision'. There has recently been reference made by government ministers to the 'need for big hitters'. The enthusiasm for elected mayors from successive governments embodies a belief in the superiority of individual leadership. The legislation to strengthen the role of non-mayoral leaders (Local Government Act 2007) giving them almost equivalent powers to those enjoyed by elected mayors (security of tenure and powers to select cabinet colleagues and allocate port-folios) highlights the belief that concentration of power is an important element of 'strong leadership'. The introduction of directly elected police commissioners in 2012 is a further example of such beliefs.

Although the term 'charisma' has rarely been incorporated into official documents, it forms another element of the governmental vision. 'A Boris in every city!' was a misguided hope expressed by David Cameron in the run-up to the referenda in 2012, on whether the public wanted elected mayors in ten of England's largest cities (in all but one case they didn't!). Whatever other qualities Boris Johnson may possess, 'charisma' would be widely seen as one of them, a view equally applicable to his predecessor at the Greater London Authority (GLA), Ken Livingstone.

Conventional wisdom about the merits of strong leadership deserves more challenge than it has recently received. There is an anomaly in the ODPM quotation above. Is 'strong leadership' necessarily effective? Can leadership that is not 'strong' (as described by the government) nevertheless prove effective in certain circumstances?

Much helpful insight into these issues is to be found in Brown's (2014) book that begins by rightly pointing out the pre-emptive nature of the idea of strong leadership:

> No-one ever says 'What we need is a weak leader'. Strength is to be admired, weakness to be deplored or pitied. Yet the facile weak-strong dichotomy is a very limited and unhelpful way of assessing individual leaders. There are many qualities desirable in a leader that should matter more than the criterion of strength … including integrity, intelligence, articulateness, shrewd judgement and courage.
>
> *(p1)*

Much has been made by enthusiasts for elected mayors of the importance of visibility. On average elected mayors enjoy a higher level of local public recognition than non-mayoral council leaders. But the reality is that outside the GLA, some council leaders have been just as recognisable and visible as their mayoral counterparts: for example, Richard Leese in Manchester, and Albert Bore in Birmingham, compared with their relatively unknown mayoral counterparts in Salford or Doncaster.

Brown's (2014) book is based on an analysis of the powers, behaviour, and effectiveness of a large number of national leaders in a wide range of different countries and political regimes. But his conclusions are equally applicable to British local government. For example:

> Far more desirable than the model of political leader as master is 'collective leadership'. Placing great power in the hands of one person is inappropriate in a democracy, and it would be an unusually lack-lustre government in which just one individual was best qualified to have the last word on everything.
>
> *(p2)*

> In democracies, collective leadership is exercised by political parties. Although parties often get a bad name, and their membership has greatly declined in most countries over the past half-century, they remain indispensable to the working of democracy, offering some policy coherence, significant political choice, and a measure of accountability.
>
> *(p9)*

> Different situations call for different styles and qualities of leadership. Thus 'the most effective leader in a given context is the group member who is best equipped to assist the group in achieving its objectives. A leader is someone who helps a group create and achieve shared goals.'
>
> *(p354)*

In these quotations, and throughout the book, Brown (2014) helpfully notes the merits of collective leadership, the sharing of leadership tasks, and the interdependent relationship between leadership groups and political parties, all of which are often ignored by the enthusiasts for strong leaders and elected mayors with a wide range of individual powers. His analysis highlights the way in which leadership styles vary between areas and over time, as different skills are required in different circumstances.

He is also critical of the positive view of personal charisma often found in such enthusiasts:

> For Weber, the concept of charisma was value-neutral. Charismatic leaders may indeed do appalling harm or great good ... moreover the idea that charisma is a special quality a leader is born with needs to be severely qualified. To a large extent, it is followers who bestow charisma on leaders, when that person seems to embody qualities they are looking for ... charismatic leadership can be won and lost, and is not generally a lifetime endowment. It is often dangerous and frequently overrated.
>
> *(p4)*

Brown prefers the term 'inspirational leadership', which he acknowledges was needed and provided most effectively by Winston Churchill in World War II. Churchill was succeeded as prime minister in 1945 by the palpably uncharismatic but equally effective Clement Attlee, whose particular strength in Brown's view was 'to enable a team of ministers with hard-earned life experience to get on with the job and to preside over the co-ordination of their efforts'. Attlee was clearly not a 'strong leader' in the current use of the term, but he was an extremely effective one.

The crucial difference between 'strong' and 'effective' leadership was highlighted in some research commissioned by the Joseph Rowntree Trust (*Local Political Leadership in Britain* by Leach et al 2004). Using the Audit Commission-derived Comprehensive Performance Assessment (CPA) ratings of the level of perceived performance in all authorities as a criterion for effective leadership, the research found that mayoral-led authorities performed no better than those lacking a mayor. It found examples of highly rated authorities where collective leadership operated, or where leadership tasks were distributed amongst a leadership group. It concluded that effective leadership came in a variety of guises, several of which would not fit the conventional wisdom of the importance of the 'strong leader'.

In these circumstances the government's desire to see the spread of elected mayors, and its enthusiasm for what it sees as 'strong leadership', are both unjustified. If authorities want to experiment with elected mayors, that's fine, but they should not be imposed, nor used as a bribe, as the government has recently done in the negotiations with the Greater Manchester combined Authority, and others. Much more desirable is to allow each individual local authority to decide which model of leadership best fits its aims, circumstances, and political culture.

If directly elected mayors are such a good idea, it is odd that an equivalent form of government at national level – a presidential system – has never been seriously considered. If strong charismatic individual leadership is the preferred model for local government, why should a presidential system not be advocated for the UK? One might reasonably expect some consistency of approach from the government.

The reason that it hasn't been seriously discussed, let alone adopted, is that all the major parties are well aware of the shortcomings of a presidential system in a climate of adversarial party politics, well illustrated by the frustrations of Barack Obama in seeking to implement his manifesto commitments (for example, radical improvements to healthcare) in the face of a hostile Republican-dominated Senate and House of Representatives.

The last two general elections in Britain (2010 and 2015) have been close enough to produce an outcome where an elected president (for example, David Cameron) could have been faced by a parliament where another political group (or cooperating groups) held a majority of the seats. In this case he would have been faced with the same kind of obstruction experienced by Barack Obama. A similar impasse occurred in those English local authorities that have held mayoral and council elections at the same time. At various times in the recent past North Tyneside, Stoke-on-Trent, and Bedford have had to find a way of dealing with a situation in which mayor and council have been elected on different manifesto commitments (and, hence, with different priorities), both of which have a degree of democratic legitimacy.

The elected-mayor model blurs the transparency of the accountability link inherent in a non-mayoral system, where in local as in general elections, parties compete with one another for election on the basis of statements of intent (manifestos) that can be evaluated by voters assessing which packet of commitments fits best (or least badly) with their own preferences.

In these circumstances the insistence of George Osborne that groups of local authorities operating as Combined Authorities in the metropolitan areas and elsewhere must accept the introduction of an elected mayor if they are to receive the full range of devolutionary benefits on offer is hard to justify. There are advantages for government ministers (and senior civil servants) in having a single individual with whom to negotiate (and to seek to hold to account, although the accountability of an elected mayor is surely to the local population). But the administrative convenience of central government should not take precedence over the democratic viability of local government.

There appears to be no recognition in central government of the shortcomings of the elected-mayor model. A single leader cannot be as representative of complex differentiated areas as can a multi-member cabinet; nor can public policies be adequately determined by just one leader – they need to be examined through the perspectives of a group of cabinet members.

There is an additional problem in the Combined Authorities that, unlike the Greater London Authority, and the 16 councils headed by an elected mayor, the mayor will be elected not to a local authority per se, but to what is in effect a multi-purpose 'joint authority', where his or her mandate will compete with the mandates of the leaders of the constituent councils of the Combined Authority (ten of them in Greater Manchester!). The lines of accountability in these circumstances become blurred, not to say opaque.

The health of local democracy

The increasing tendency for the centre to intervene in the structures and processes of local decision-making has been influenced by a set of linked worries about the health of local democracy, of which the concern to strengthen local political leadership is but one response. There is a prevalent, media-fuelled view that is critical of the current state of local politics and local democracy. All too often, one encounters in the media an unprepossessing caricature of local democracy that is viewed as a justification for central intervention. Local democracy, it is asserted, has atrophied because of the low calibre of local councillors, who typically behave in a parochial fashion, and vote themselves inflated levels of allowances. There is too much party politics, with an unnecessary imposition of group discipline on a range of issues that would be better decided on their merits. It is not surprising (or so it is claimed) that turnout at local elections is so low, or that voters typically use local elections to express their view of national parties and issues rather than local concerns. In these circumstances, because the democratic legitimacy of local government is perceived to be so low, it is seen as acceptable for central government to intervene in the public interest.

We are not claiming that this caricature represents the official position of this (or earlier) governments, although there is evidence that it forms part of the assumptive world of civil servants and some (but not all) government ministers (see Jones and Travers 1994). Several of these concerns can equally be applied to the state of democracy at the national level, where party politics is also dominant, MPs frequently behave in a similarly parochial fashion where constituency matters are concerned (for example, local hospital closures) and election turnout rates have declined more sharply in general elections since 1997 than they have at local level (where they have remained relatively stable). There is a powerful alternative explanation for the failing health of local democracy, namely one that has its roots in the greatly reduced scope for local choice by local councils, which has developed over the past 30 years, and the consequent decline in councillor recruitment and motivation, and the level of public interest.

The role of political parties

Let us first examine the criticism that party politics is over-dominant in local government. It is important to recognise that the critical public view of party politics has developed most forcibly over its role in national government, rather than at the local level.

Political parties, or at least the principal parties currently represented in parliament (Scottish Nationalists excepted), are inciting cynicism, criticism, and apathy amongst the electorate. They have increasingly been seen as both lacking in the capacity to meet the challenges facing Britain, and undemocratic, in their tendency to rely on spin, over-the-top discipline via the party whips, being constantly 'on message', and indulging in vacuous political posturing in parliamentary debates and prime minister's question time. The recent exposure of the business dealings of two former home secretaries, Jack Straw and Sir Malcolm Rifkind, has added further fuel to the fire of public hostility, whether or not their behaviour has actually 'broken the rules', given that the MPs expenses scandal of 2009–2010 is recent enough not to have been forgotten.

Although councillors have continued to enjoy higher levels of public trust than do MPs, the operation of party politics in local government has by no means been immune from this negative public perception, an outcome intensified by the recent revelations in Rotherham (failure to protect vulnerable children) and Tower Hamlets (vote-rigging). The rigidity of party discipline, the ritual inter-party conflict at council meetings and the unrealistic promises made in local-election manifestos have all been viewed as evidence of the Westminster malaise at the local level.

So, would local government be in a healthier state if party representation and politics were absent or (more realistically) greatly diminished in local authorities? That is certainly the view of the independents who are now in the ascendancy on Frome Town Council. In 2011 a group of local activists, disillusioned with the dominance of political parties on the council, decided to come together as a new grouping called Independents for Frome (IfF), and went on to contest all 17 council seats, 10 of which they won. Mac-Fadyen (2014, pp3–4) provides a stimulating analysis of the reasons why the grouping was formed, what tactics they used in the run-up to the election, and what they have achieved. He concludes:

> In our experience, at local levels of representation, party politics as practised by the current political parties are an irrelevant and corrosive diversion ... Britain today operates a dysfunctional political system.

In many ways what has happened in Frome is encouraging. IfF seems to have succeeded in reviving public interest in the local council (previously an inactive, unresponsive party-dominated entity) in a sizeable town (Frome has a population of approximately 27,000). They have a good record in opening up its decision-making processes to local involvement and influence, and have several substantive achievements on the ground to their credit. They appear to be achieving their underlying aim of 'making politics relevant, effective and fun'. If what has happened in Frome were to be replicated in similar-sized towns across the country, we would indeed be experiencing a reinvigoration of local democracy, with some prospect that it would in due course permeate the world of national politics.

However, one is left with a number of reservations about the scope for replicating the Frome experience at governmental levels beyond the town or parish council. Politics, whether party or non-party-based, is inherent in any public body with responsibility for allocating resources and public goods, deciding who gets what, when, where, and how. IfF is necessarily operating politically, whether or not its adherents recognise it. At the level of a town council, with a revenue budget of UK£1 million, it may be possible to resolve differences between the priorities, demands, needs, and interests of local residents in the open participatory way (without the need for party politics). But as you move up governmental levels to Mendip District Council (within which Frome is located) and Somerset County Council this approach becomes more problematical. MacFadyen makes several references to 'putting the needs of the community first' and 'doing what is best for the community'. But the 'community', even in Frome and certainly at district and county level, is not undifferentiated. There will exist a range of different interests, based on differences in income, social class, age, ethnicity, and location, to name but five. The job of politics is to recognise these differences and to make judgements about priorities, in the knowledge that some interests will necessarily be favoured more than (or at the expense of) others. One of the strengths of party politics is that parties can put forward a coherent interlinked set of priorities, based on different political philosophies, which will necessarily give more priority to some interests than others. Voters can then choose between a range of different value-imbued options (typically set out in manifestos). The fact that many voters do not behave rationally, in that they do not weigh, compare, and evaluate these different value statements, does not detract from their importance in the democratic process. As Brown (2014) argues, even though parties often get a bad name, they remain indispensable to the working of democracy, offering some policy coherence, significant political choice, and a measure of accountability. At territorial levels wider than the Fromes of this world, political parties provide a basis for informed democratic choice, which it would be difficult to replicate in a fundamentally different form. A party-based system has its imperfections and shortcomings, particularly apparent at the present time. But it's difficult to envisage a viable democratic alternative.

Some of the problems of councils dominated by independents were apparent in a council with which one of the authors worked some years ago. What is the strategy of the independent group (which dominated the council) the chief executive was asked. 'They don't have one,' he replied. 'They ask me to come up with proposals, and then tell me whether or not they like them!' What we have here is a recipe for ad hoc decision-making, lack of direction, and officer-domination, none of which are desirable democratic attributes.

It sounds as if the Frome independents are better organised and more proactive than many of their counterparts elsewhere, so much so that you could argue that they operate as a de facto political party. They may behave in ways that are refreshingly free from the group discipline, political points-scoring, and closed-mindedness of the traditional parties (at their worst). But they have developed a coherent programme – a vision for Frome – which is rightly vulnerable at the next election to challenge from other, competing local visions, some of which will no doubt reflect party philosophies.

It is difficult to imagine how a world of local government free of party politics could present the electorate with meaningful strategic choices about a town, city, or county's future. But it would be a healthy democratic development if the major parties operating in local government were prepared to reconsider the way that they operate, and move away from the rigidities of their current modus operandi.

Hence, in our view the challenge is not to seek to diminish the role of political parties in local government, although where independent groups do emerge and win seats as they do from time to time it is often a healthy development in response to a stagnant one party-dominated political culture. The challenge is to find ways of strengthening the democratic viability and public responsiveness of parties in local government. Such an agenda would seek to improve local electoral processes, the representativeness of local parties, and the post-election responsiveness of party groups to public participation.

It would be difficult and inappropriate to seek to legislate on these issues, which are primarily the responsibility of political parties themselves, both nationally and locally. If they are prepared to improve processes for local candidate selection (including seeking to provide a more representative group of candidates in age, sex, ethnicity, and class), for the drawing-up of local manifestos, for the stimulation of and responsiveness to public engagement, and for improving the quality of inter-party debate in public meetings (ideally by being more flexible, where appropriate, in the use of party discipline), then local democracy will flourish. Increased devolution of local decision-making to local councils would also help.

Political management structures: what needs to change

The current pattern of political-management arrangements in England is nearly as replete with inconsistencies as is territorial structure. Councils have been strongly encouraged by successive governments to adopt the elected mayor model, but relatively few (currently 17, including the GLA) have yet done so. Elected mayors have not caught the public's imagination. In two-thirds of the referenda under the previous Labour governments, local people voted against the introduction of an elected mayor. In the ten 'big city' referenda held in May 2012, only Bristol voted in favour (though Doncaster voted to retain an elected mayor, unlike Hartlepool who, shortly afterwards, did not). Currently, the introduction of mayoral government does not require a referendum. Any council wishing to can do so, if there is a simple majority of the council in favour of the idea, as has happened recently in Leicester, Liverpool, and Salford. But the fact that so few councils have taken advantage of this opportunity indicates there is little support for elected mayors within councils, as well as amongst local populations.

Elsewhere in England, the dominant model is the leader and cabinet system, which 83 per cent of all councils introduced in 2000, following the Local Government Act. Authorities with populations under 85,000 had the option under that act of retaining the traditional committee system (albeit in streamlined form), which 13 per cent choose to do. Currently any (non-mayoral) council that wishes to revert to a committee system may do so, on a majority vote of the council. Nottinghamshire County Council is amongst the few to have done so.

Earlier in this chapter we provided a critique of the current fashion within government circles for elected mayors. Our view is that while elected mayors have some important advantages, not least public recognition within their areas and level of credibility (and, hence, influence) with external partners, we are less convinced than Simon Jenkins (and others) that the advantages necessarily outweigh the disadvantages. The emphasis on individual charismatic leadership, which both the current and previous governments have enthusiastically espoused, is not an intrinsically 'better' form of leadership than collective collegiate models, except in visibility. The diffusion of power is of potential value within local authorities as elsewhere – just as the concentration of power in one individual has potential dangers. Collective forms of leadership can operate just as effectively as individualised leadership. And the mayoral model, as it is currently promulgated, seems to reflect the government's policy focus on economic development and growth, primarily in conurbations, cities, and large towns, rather than across the country as a whole.

The choice of political-management arrangements is one that should most appropriately be left to each local authority and its citizens. The principle of subsidiarity should apply in relation to this issue, as with many other choices. There is no 'national interest' at stake in insisting on a particular decision-making model (or a limited choice of such models).

We see no reason why a local authority should not be free to change from one form of decision-making structure to another. But there would be a case for maintaining, as a safeguard against party-political opportunism, the current practice that a referendum is required before a council can change its governing arrangements, whether to or from a mayor, to ensure that the proposed changes involve public engagement and debate before a decision is made.

Simon Jenkins's proposal that 'mayors' could be elected from within the council, as head of a collective cabinet, as in France and Belgium, would not really involve a significant departure from current practice in the way in which a council leader is elected and empowered. But if the use of the term 'elected mayor' has the status with external partners that it appears to have, then local authorities should certainly be permitted to operate on this basis. We think this mayoral option would generate more widespread enthusiasm within councils, because it involves much less change to traditional practices, and should not need the backing of a referendum.

The appeal of becoming a candidate in a local election could be enhanced if local authorities were prepared to improve the effectiveness of the scrutiny function (otherwise known as overview and scrutiny) that would also have the effect of strengthening their accountability. Scrutiny committees (or panels), introduced in the 2000 Local Government Act primarily to hold the newly empowered local executives to account, have struggled to make an impact. They have often been seen by 'backbench' members as a poor substitute for the traditional pre-2000 service committees, and, with no power of decision-making, and their contribution can easily be disregarded by unsympathetic executives. Yet, the contribution to parliamentary accountability made by the Select Committees at their best (for example, as chaired by Margaret Hodge, Tony Wright, and the late Gwyneth Dunwoody) show what can be achieved, especially when high-profile issues (such as HSBC banking practices) are investigated. Select Committee procedures provide one possible model (amongst many others) from which scrutiny committees can choose. A crucial ingredient for effective scrutiny (at both governmental levels) is independent support from officers who can dig out evidence that enables scrutiny committee members to challenge portfolio holders and chief officers. Rotherham MBC might have emerged with less discredit from its failure to protect vulnerable children from sexual exploitation if a scrutiny committee had earlier picked up that there was a problem and had decided to investigate it. Currently, the impact of austerity on council budgets leaves little scope to strengthen scrutiny support units. But if and when greater financial room for manoeuvre returns, local authorities might usefully enhance their scrutiny and overview functions.

Choice of electoral systems

There are four main alternative forms of electoral system that merit consideration in any discussion aimed at strengthening the democratic basis of local government, namely:

- a continuation of the existing first past the post (FPTP) system;
- 'majority systems' – for example, the Alternative Vote, the main aim of which is to eliminate the possibility of a candidate winning a constituency on a minority vote;
- a proportional representation system, which aims to achieve proportionality between votes cast and seats won – the two principle variants of

this system being the Single Transferable Vote (STV) and the Party List system;

- hybrid systems, typically based on FPTP, but with some amendment or 'top up', aimed at achieving a higher degree of proportionality in the elected body as a whole.

All of these systems have democratic strengths and weaknesses, which we consider below.

First past the post

A key strength of FPTP is that it is supportive of a constituency-based system, at a relatively localised level. The arguments for retaining some form of constituency- (or ward-) based system are persuasive, and less easily facilitated by other electoral systems.

The democratic arguments for a system in which local people can contact a councillor who has a mandate to 'speak for' the local area concerned and the residents within it are formidable. This system operates at Westminster, and we are not aware of any convincing arguments as to why it should not continue at the local as well as the central level. Recent parliamentary debate has been about the size and definition of constituency boundaries, not the principle of a constituency-based system. The link between local elections, local councillors, and local people has always been at the heart of local democratic practice, and should remain so.

But there is a major democratic shortcoming in a wholly constituency-based system. Individual voters have to express a single preference that encompasses choices between both individuals and parties. If they have a strong (or even reasonably strong) party preference, they are likely to vote for whoever represents that party, irrespective of his or her record (or potential) as a good ward councillor. There will, however, sometimes be circumstances where voters are pulled in different directions (party or quality of local representative?) and have to decide which criterion to give preference to.

The dominance of party-based voting at local level (reflected in the long-term decline of independent councillors) in a first past the post (FPTP) electoral system can produce outcomes that appear distinctly 'undemocratic'. There have been instances where every single seat on a council has been won by one particular party, even though its share of the overall vote has been little over 50 per cent. There have been instances where a party has polled 25 per cent of the popular vote and not won a single seat. Neither of these outcomes are justifiable democratically. Local voters need party representation on the council as well as good individual ward representatives. If 45 per cent of the population didn't vote Labour in Newham, the fact that they have no party representation on the council seems, on the face of it, democratically unsustainable.

Majority and PR systems

The potential value of all the other systems is that they would invariably increase proportionality, that is involve a closer match between the preferences expressed by electors and the composition of the council. However, the alternative vote is weakest in this respect.

The use of the AV would usually make some contribution to increased proportionality, although not necessarily very much. The single transferable vote (STV) would provide the closest match between voter preferences and council composition, but would require much larger constituencies, which would dilute the democratic advantages of a constituency-based system, and be much more likely to result in hung councils, an outcome that itself has democratic advantages and disadvantages. Other options would rely on some form of 'top-up' system, which could be used to adjust the overall political composition of the council to provide a closer (although by no means perfect) approximation to the distribution of votes cast for the different parties.

One form of top-up mechanism is the Party List system. But there are drawbacks to the use of list systems in local elections. It depersonalises the voting process, and relies too heavily on party-based criteria for prioritising the names on the list (which may not necessarily equate with the most potentially effective candidates).

The potential advantage of a hybrid system is that it could incorporate a mechanism to enhance proportionality, without undermining the advantages of a constituency-based system. But the form of this system that operates in elections to the Scottish Assembly relies on a Party List system to top-up the outcome of the FPTP constituency-based elections. Are there any alternatives that can be identified?

One alternative would be to include in the quota those unsuccessful candidates in the FPTP election from the qualifying parties who gained the largest proportion of votes but failed to get elected. In this way, the top-up councillors would have a degree of democratic legitimacy, which could not be claimed by those who owed their election to their position on the party list.

If this alternative were to be adopted, two questions remain. On what basis should the 'top-up' quota of seats be allocated? And what proportion of council seats should be allocated through ward-based elections and the top-up process respectively? All of the alternatives to FPTP (with the possible exception of AV) increase the probability of the election resulting in a hung authority. Could this outcome be seen as unqualifiedly healthy and desirable in democratic terms, or is this view open to challenge?

Hung authorities have since the 1980s become an established part of the political landscape of Britain, even under a wholly FPTP constituency-based electoral system. The proportion of hung authorities has varied over the past three decades, but it has sometimes been as high as one in three of all British local authorities. Since the change in the local electoral system in Scotland, where the single transferable vote (STV) system was introduced in 2007, hung authorities have become the norm. Only seven authorities are currently in majority control (and three of those are the independent island authorities).

There are many advantages to hung authorities: they put pressure on different parties to seek common ground, the outcomes of council debates are less predictable, and they avoid the possibility of extremism, either of the right or the left. There is no evidence that hung authorities have performed any less well than those with majority-control (on the basis of CPA and other data).

The democratic downside to hung authorities, particularly those that are run by a coalition, is that they tend to obscure the process of choice in local elections. In a majority-controlled council the dominant party has been returned on the basis of a manifesto, which it then seeks to implement. In due course voters can make a judgement as to how the majority party has performed (including the extent to which it has delivered on its manifesto commitments) and make an informed choice as to how they wish to vote at the next election. This feature has been an opportunity at almost all general elections from 1950 onwards (although we are not claiming that every voter necessarily exercises his or her choice in this rational way!).

In a coalition both parties will have had to negotiate compromises over their manifesto commitments. Once they have been achieved, it is likely that they will wish to present a 'united front' to press and public (c.f. the 2010 national coalition government). In judging performance at the next election, it may be difficult for voters to disentangle which party has been (largely) responsible for what (indeed, in the 2015 general election voters were faced with this very problem). In hung authorities where all three major parties are cooperating, it will be even more difficult.

Hence, there are problems over the transparency of the democratic-choice process in many (although by no means all) hung authorities (transparency and 'holding to account' are less problematical in 'minority' administrations). Hung authorities have advantages and there is certainly no need to fear this outcome, but the advantages do not necessarily outweigh the disadvantages, especially as the basis for rational electoral choice. Would it be democratically healthy if, as a result of increasing proportionality through STV or some form of hybrid system, the vast majority of local authorities in England ended up with no overall control, which is the outcome that currently prevails in Scotland local authorities?

Depending upon what balance was sought between the democratic benefits of proportionality and majority control, respectively, one option would be to introduce a hybrid system in which a significant majority of council seats – perhaps two-thirds – would be subject to FPTP ward-based elections, while the remaining one-third should be distributed on the basis of the overall proportion of votes cast for the different parties at the election. This approach would reduce the large majorities that are currently commonplace in local authorities, but not in a way that transforms the vast majority of them into hung councils.

This book is not a detailed blueprint for reform, and we would not presume to make a firm proposal as to which electoral system should be introduced. But it is important that the democratic advantages and disadvantages of the various options should be set down and understood, before action is taken, which is what we have sought to do here. And the democratic advantages of permitting councils to develop their own proposals for changes in their electoral systems and then presenting them in a referendum for public approval (or otherwise) should also be borne in mind.

Council size and constituency definition

There is at present little consistency in the size of councils. There has been a move recently to argue for reductions in council size, which has been justified on the basis of significant reductions in council responsibilities over the past 30 years, and in the resulting reduction in the scope for genuine local choice. There have also been unsubstantiated claims about diminishing 'councillor calibre', which, even if true, would be most likely to reflect the reduction in status (although not the time demands) of the job over the same period of time.

Building from the bottom up, a population of 5000 is about the right constituency size in terms of workload generation, although significant variation around this figure would be acceptable to respond to considerations of local community identity. Although middle-class areas experience less in the way of social and economic problems than more deprived areas, their populations are usually more articulate; hence in workload, there is no need to vary ward size to take account of socio-economic differences. There is little justification for multi-member wards, and to introduce (or retain) them would under our proposals produce inappropriately large councils. For the larger counties and cities, combinations of two (or more) units of 5000 might be necessary to keep council size at a reasonable level (for example, in councils such as Birmingham and Kent).

Electoral frequency

Finally, there is the issue of electoral frequency. Again there is little consistency in the present arrangements. While in some types of council (county councils, London boroughs) a four-year electoral cycle is a requirement, in others (metropolitan boroughs) the requirement is for elections three years out of four; shire districts and unitary authorities can choose which of these two alternatives to operate.

Although in other respects we have advocated allowing local authorities to make their own choices (for example, on political-management systems), which may also be appropriate for electoral frequency, there is a case to be considered for the introduction of a more uniform pattern. The arguments for more or less frequent elections are well known. More frequent elections give more opportunity for local people to express a view about the performance of parties and councillors (and help to sustain the activity of local political parties). Less frequent elections give more time for the successful party or parties to implement their priorities, without having to take account of a further election approaching within a year. In some authorities this electoral frequency is a recipe for political instability and frequent upheaval.

Central government would not dream of introducing annual elections, and, in our view, the arguments against doing so are equally relevant at the local level. As well as the potential for instability, annual elections create barriers to informed judgements about the performance of a new administration (which will in its first year be implementing a budget not of its choosing). However, electoral frequency is an issue that could and perhaps should be a matter of local choice.

All of these issues are important, but they are less urgent than those of constitutional safeguarding, financial arrangements, and the allocation of service responsibilities, which have been covered in Chapters 5 and 6. There are no 'right answers'. Questions such as 'what is the most appropriate system for local elections' and 'how large councils should be' have concerned policy-makers and academics over a long period of time, generating much disagreement and little in the way of consensus. What we have tried to do here is to explore and evaluate the various options.

8

CENTRAL–LOCAL RELATIONS AND LOCAL-GOVERNMENT REORGANISATION

Introduction

The history of the territorial reorganisation of local government over the past 50 years illustrates a number of key features of the central–local relationship. It highlights what can happen in the absence of a formal constitution (or, failing that, a statutory code of conduct that could be used to challenge arbitrary central-government initiatives). It demonstrates the dominance of the 'service-provision' model of local government in the 'mind-set' of the centre (shared by both ministers and senior civil servants). It provides a powerful example of a dominant narrative, which has developed in the minds of many local chief executives and leaders, as well as the centre, into a conventional wisdom. As we point out below, in the past 50 years there have been a series of reorganisations imposed on local government for reasons that owe more to political expediency or initiative than rational justification.

But does it really matter what kind of structure prevails in local government? In Chapter 6 it was argued that a variety of political-management structures can and have been made to work. The same is true of territorial structures. Following a reorganisation, the new authorities, after a period of transition, adjust to the new circumstances and do what is expected of them in much the same way as did their predecessors. The difference lies in the fact that while members of the public have little interest in political-management structures (witness the low voter turnout in the elected-mayor referenda), they often have considerable interest in the way that the authority in which they live is defined. Examples include the high level of public pressure to preserve Rutland, to extract Herefordshire from its forced 1975 marriage with Worcestershire, and to sever the connection between Lancaster and Morecambe (in the mid-1990s the Morecambe Bay Independents were the largest group in Lancaster City Council). These and many other examples all demonstrate the importance to local people of inhabiting authorities that match their sense of community. If governments – central or local – are concerned, as they should be, to strengthen community development and involvement, then it is important that their territorial definitions correspond as far as possible close to people's own perceptions of community identity.

Fifty years of local-government reorganisation

The structure of local government established in the 1880s and 1890s (counties, county boroughs, the London County Council, London boroughs, municipal boroughs, urban and rural districts) survived more or less intact for more than 70 years. Any changes made were marginal, and usually involved the awarding of county borough status to fast-expanding municipal boroughs. When in the late 1950s and 1960s it was recognised that there was a strong case for structural change, influenced by the car-dominated journey-to-work patterns around the nuclei of cities and large towns, then the governments of the day established Royal Commissions to examine evidence and make recommendations (the Herbert Commission on Greater London, 1960; the Redcliffe-Maud Commission for England, 1969; the Wheatley Commission in Scotland, 1969). This approach was an acknowledgement that changes of this nature were matters of 'constitutional' significance. All three commissions presented a set of coherent proposals that were largely accepted in the case of the Herbert and Wheatley Commissions. However, the 1970–1974 Conservative government modified the recommendations of the Redcliffe-Maud Commission, although the two-tier structure it established in both metropolitan and shire areas (with a different allocation of functions between the counties and districts concerned) did have a reasonable degree of logic and consistency about it.

This awareness that local-government reorganisations should be dealt with in a quasi-constitutional manner was then increasingly side-lined by a series of ad hoc interventions in the structures established in 1966 and 1974, which owed more to party political (and civil service) interests than they did to evidence-based analysis. Collectively, they have had a destabilising influence on local government.

The response of the 1974–1979 Labour government to the loss in status of about 20 large- to medium-sized cities that had before 1974 been 'all-purpose' county boroughs (and that were more often than not Labour-controlled) set in motion this drift towards destabilisation. A White Paper misleadingly entitled *Organic Change* (Department of the Environment 1979) set out proposals for transferring education and social services back to these cities. This policy initiative fell by the wayside when Labour lost the 1979 election, but the precedent had been set and the damage done.

The next disruption came in 1983 when the Conservative government, indignant at the high-profile political activities of the Livingstone-led Greater London Council, decided to abolish it (and the six metropolitan county councils that were set up in 1974). The White Paper that introduced the change – *Streamlining the Cities* (HMSO 1983) – was one of the least convincing examples of the genre ever written. But despite the strength of the opposition, both inside and outside Parliament, the measure was passed and in 1986 the 32 London boroughs and 36 metropolitan district councils became so-called 'unitary authorities'. This nomenclature ignored the plethora of joint boards and joint committees that were established in all seven of these areas to carry out the functions (police, fire, public transport, waste disposal) that couldn't, in reality, be devolved directly to the borough or district councils. The later abolition of the Inner London Education Authority (ILEA) in 1989 was similarly politically motivated.

In 1991 the developing pattern of arbitrary politically-inspired central government tinkering with local-government structure received a further boost. Michael Heseltine was faced with the need to devise a framework that abolished the poll tax, but chose to introduce a more wide-ranging policy rationale for doing so, to mask the transparency of the policy U-turn. The rationale was a so-called 'root-and-branch' review of the functions, structure, and financing of local government. In reality, the review proved to be much more limited in scope than it was first presented, but it did lead to the establishment of the Local Government Commission (chaired by John Banham), which was charged with the task of making recommendations for changes in local-government structure in the shire areas, with a clear presumption in favour of unitary authorities. This steer was not supported by rational argument in the commission's guidelines; it is likely that it resulted from the simplistic assumption that now that unitary authorities had been created in the metropolitan areas, there was no reason not to extend their introduction to other parts of the country. The 'unitary is best' dominant narrative was gaining momentum, without ever having been challenged or tested.

The Banham Commission, demonstrating unexpected qualities of independence and courage, refused to make unitary recommendations where it felt that evidence (particularly that of public opinion) did not justify it. By 1996 at the end of the process, a further 46 unitary authorities had been established, many fewer than would have been forecast at the start.

The most recent unitary-inspired policy initiative was the most unsatisfactory and bizarre of the whole series. The White Paper *Strong and Prosperous Communities* (DCLG 2006) included the provision that councils would be invited to submit bids to become unitary authorities. This time there was no apparent political imperative behind the initiative. Chisholm and Leach (2008) argue that the most likely explanation for its introduction was the change of minister half-way through the drafting of the White Paper, with the new, inexperienced minister, Ruth Kelly, proving vulnerable to civil service advice, which was by now pro-unitary. Despite the blatant inconsistencies involved in the government's response to the bids, a further ten unitary authorities were set up, most of them county-based, with relative large (average 300,000–400,000) populations. Large unitary authorities had become the conventional wisdom, without a convincing case having been made for them, other than by the Redcliffe-Maud Commission who considered the county borough to be the most effective of all structures, and recommended unitary authorities in all areas other than the three major provincial conurbations centred on Manchester, Liverpool, and Birmingham.

Although for most of the 2010–2015 coalition government's period of office, local-government structure was not subjected to further tinkering, a few months before the 2015 election there was a development that was on the face of it encouraging, but also perplexing. The Chancellor George Osborne announced in November 2014 that he had agreed a devolution deal with the Greater Manchester Combined Authority (which comprises the ten metropolitan district councils that covers the former area of Greater Manchester County Council, which was abolished in 1986). In what came to be known as the 'Northern Powerhouse' initiative, several blocks of central-government expenditure, including economic development, public transport, and (a particular surprise) health were to be devolved in 2016 to the Combined Authority. A condition was attached, namely that the ten authorities must agree to the introduction of a directly elected mayor (with a transition period when the mayor was elected by the councils involved). Although this initiative, which is to be replicated in other metropolitan areas (and indeed elsewhere), does not involve a formal restructuring, it implies a de facto reintroduction of metropolitan counties, albeit in an indirectly rather than directly elected basis. It also involves the first evidence of central–local devolution for a long time. We discuss both aspects in more detail later in this chapter and in Chapter 9.

Local-government reorganisation; technocratic, and democratic perspectives

In Chapter 1 it was argued that two 'alternative' conceptions of the purpose of local government can be identified, which have been allocated different priority throughout its history. First, there is the assumption that the key purpose of local government is to deliver, coordinate, and prioritise local services, in accordance with national requirements. But there is an alternative view of what local government is primarily there to do: a 'governmental' model, involving the identification of and response to the full range of problems, challenges, and opportunities facing a locality. These two key purposes are not incompatible, but it is important to be clear which is perceived as dominant.

If the fundamental purpose of local authorities is to provide, commission, or administer a range of services in line with criteria established by the centre (class size, curriculum content, benefits administration, planning control), then 'economies of scale' arguments are at least potentially relevant, even if the validity of the arguments has been disputed, and are, in any event, biased by ignoring diseconomies of scale. But if the fundamental purpose is a governmental one, then other criteria, notably community identity, become increasingly relevant, and typically pull in the opposite direction to the possibility of service-related economics of scale.

Copus (2006, p6) argues that the (misguided) assumption that 'bigger is better' reflects a *technocratic* model of local government as opposed to a *democratic* model, which would focus on the opportunities for civic involvement at a level meaningful to local people:

> Technocracy, with its focus on service management, administration, efficiency and effectiveness … requires even larger units of local government, based on the perception that such bigger units are inherently more efficient and effective when it comes to the delivery of public services. [This] argument is based on the mistaken assumption that the

economies of scale that accrue to large units of private enterprise will necessarily accrue to the public sector; a sector not driven by the profit motive. Democracy, on the other hand, particularly local democracy, flourishes where small units of government are concerned, where cohesive communities can be identified and represented, and their views responded to, and indeed, where experiments with direct democracy can clearly signal the wishes of the people to governing institutions.

The notion that local government is primarily, if not exclusively, about the provision of public services has hindered the development of English councils as politically powerful local centres of government that are meaningful and relevant to local people. Moreover, this thinking has produced in England some of the largest units of local government in Europe. Rather than representing geographically distinct and identifiable communities, many council boundaries have amalgamated a number of communities and distinct geographical areas in order to reach the size of population deemed necessary for the provision of efficient and effective public services.

The increasing influence of the technocratic model on local-government reorganisations has caused a disjuncture between councils and communities and, ironically, a central concern about levels of engagement between them. If councils are to be locally meaningful entities, reflecting a popular perception of a place, then their definition needs to reflect that shared perception of place, rather than the outcome of administrative convenience.

The detachment of reorganisation outcomes from community identity

Nowhere is the disjunction between the territorial definition of councils and popular perception of place better illustrated than in the names that have been given to new councils from 1974 onwards. When central government has merged councils in reorganisations, there is a need to create a name for the 'new council' that will elicit agreement amongst the authorities merged. Easier said than done!

Traditionally, place names have reflected the physical geography of a location, its culture and history, and the people associated with it. Since the 1975 reorganisation, however, there has been a proliferation of what may be termed 'non-place' names – labels that have been manufactured to enable the new councils to begin afresh with an entirely new identity.

If one examines the current map of English local government, three categories of council names can be identified that illustrate the growing mismatch between named units of local government and recognisable geographical communities. They can be labelled: 'the point of the compass' councils, the 'and' councils, and the 'non-existent' councils (see Copus 2010, 2011).

The 'point of the compass' council is one where, in the naming process, a district has been allocated the name of the county in which it is situated, to which has been added a navigational reference point, presumably used to assist the traveller in finding the new council. Examples of these 'compass point councils' are many and varied (South Norfolk, West Berkshire, East Northamptonshire, North Kesteven, and the lucky holder of two compass point references: North East Derbyshire).

Second, there are the 'and' councils where the name of the council reflects the convenient merging of former councils and where the desire to avoid offence is solved by simply inserting the word 'and' between the names of towns, such as in the following examples: (Kings Lynn and West Norfolk; Oadby and Wigston; Epsom and Ewell; Hinckley and Bosworth).

Finally, and most indicative of the cavalier fashion with which communities are often treated when councils are merged, are the non-existent councils. The very names of these councils are simply made up, and do not reflect any geographical location. Rather, some inoffensive link to an area – no matter how tenuous – is used to give a title to the new council entity. Examples include: Three Rivers, Havering, Tendring, Broxtowe, Waverley, and Kirklees, which was formed in 1974 by merging Batley, Cleckheaton, Dewsbury, and Holmfirth with their much larger neighbour, Huddersfield. The name 'Kirklees' derives from Kirklees Priory where Robin Hood, the heroic English outlaw, is rumoured to be buried (Copus 2011)!

Such is the strength of local attachment to the councils involved in forced mergers that it is invariably the case that none of the names of the merging councils is likely to prove acceptable to the others in deciding what to call the new merged entity. Hence the search for inoffensive compromises, however artificial and meaningless to most residents that the compromises appear.

Local-authority areas have become too large to match the real places with which people identify – hence the necessity for so many councils to be place-builders and place-shapers. Councils are often left trying to forge an identity – albeit an artificial one – around often disparate communities (Tameside, Trafford, Sefton, and Sandwell provide examples; there are many others).

As a result of this cumulative move to bigger authorities, which has detached councils from place, people, culture, history, and the identities forged from tradition, councils are finding it increasingly difficult to avoid an emphasis on operating as providers or commissioners of public services, rather than as politically representative and governing institutions. An added advantage for the centre is that the more detached from real places local government units become, the easier it is to continue the policy of mergers and amalgamations producing ever-larger local-government units. One of the most important challenges in the renewal of local authorities as genuine organs of community government is to find a way of re-forging the crucial link between community identity and governmental units.

Simon Jenkins (2004, p106) was right when he argued for a return to the pre-1974 structure:

> The map of local government that existed prior to 1974 was a good one. The map survives in essence to this day and there is no good reason for tearing it up. It accepts … two tiers in rural areas of county councils and subsidiary municipalities … This is as it has been for a century past. It reflects the local sentiments and loyalties of people nationwide. It has diversity without complexity. It is proven abroad.

Explaining the drift to large unitary authorities

There is a narrative that is currently dominating public discussion about the most appropriate form and size of local authorities, which is becoming increasingly heretical to challenge, but increasingly important to do so. There are three linked elements. The first is that the predominant role of local authorities is service delivery (see above). The second is the assumption or belief that larger authorities are more cost-effective than smaller ones, and hence to be preferred. The third is that unitary authorities where there is only one principal local council within a given area (discounting parish and town councils) are preferable to a two-tier system of local government. The justifications typically used are that unitary authorities are more cost-effective (less messy duplication and overlap of service responsibilities); more conflict-free (no county/district disagreements and tension); and that a unitary system is easier for the public to understand because all services for which local government is responsible fall within the province of a single authority.

There is a further element to the narrative, perhaps less explicit than the three so far discussed, which has insidiously become part of the conventional wisdom, namely that we have 'too many' councillors in England, and a significant reduction in their numbers is desirable. Any change from a two-tier system to a unitary system (or a merger of two or more individual authorities into a larger entity) will have the effect of greatly reducing the overall number of councillors in the area. The larger the new unitary authority, the greater the level of reduction (Cornwall lost 70 per cent of its councillors when it became a unitary authority in 2008).

It might be thought that this last outcome would be seen as problematical. In the 'official mind set' of the Department for Communities and Local Government (DCLG), however, the reverse is true. The level of disdain held in central-government departments for local authorities, in general, and for councillors, in particular, has been well documented (see Jones and Travers 1994). Conversations the authors have had with civil servants (and ministers) confirm the continued prevalence of this phenomenon. Added to which, if local government is seen as primarily about the organisation and delivery (directly or indirectly) of a range of specific services, then why do we need so many councils and hence councillors (or so the argument goes). Sadly, this view is by no means absent within local authorities themselves. There is perceived to be a good deal of 'dead wood'. Councillor calibre (whatever that means) is perceived to have been reducing ever since the great days when local captains of industry, country squires, and retired admirals and majors were leaders of local authorities.

All of the assumptions underlying this narrative can be challenged. But however disputable its evidence base, the narrative has gained the status of 'common sense', incorporating a series of linked 'of course' statements. Of course, bigger unitary authorities are the best structural form. The reality is that the economies-of-scale argument is premised on the assumption that local government is primarily concerned with the provision of local services, which is a limited and one-sided perception of its role. Evidence about the greater cost-effectiveness of larger authorities compared with smaller ones is at best inconclusive, and anyway needs to be balanced by the demonstrable benefits of smaller authorities (see Chapter 1).

Given the way in which responsibilities for local services have been dispersed over the past 30 years amongst a range of different agencies, the alleged gains in public comprehension about who does what are largely illusory (and, in these circumstances, 'unitary authorities' hardly merit the 'unitary' nomenclature). A two-tier system has the value of identifying and encouraging the resolution of real differences of priority between the respective levels of local government (for example, over planning and environmental issues), which would be more likely to be suppressed in a unitary system. And the number of councillors per head of population in Britain is already well below that of any other Western democracy. Why would we want to reduce it still further? Two- or three-tier systems posed no problems for the designers of the 1966 and 1974 reorganisations. Nor are multi-tiered systems regarded as sub-optimal structures elsewhere in Europe, where they are the norm. The 'bigger is better' belief is also much less dominant in Europe. Communes representing real places remain a valued feature of the French local-government system.

So how did the current English narrative develop? It emerged on to the agenda during the politically inspired abolition of the Greater London Council (GLC) and the metropolitan county councils in 1986. The upper tier was perceived as 'wasteful'; there was nothing that the GLC and the metropolitan counties did that the London boroughs and met districts couldn't do (except, of course, that there was!). This belief was then taken up by Michael Heseltine in 1991 and was built into the terms of reference of the Banham Committee, which caused a further 46 unitary authorities to be established. This outcome set the scene for a further bout of instability. Precedents had been set and inconsistencies had become apparent, producing further instability in the local-government map of shire areas. If Derby was to become a unitary authority, then why not Norwich? If Peterborough, then why not Northampton?

Into this fluidity, there developed elements of complicity. By the 1990s there had emerged a civil service view that large unitary authorities were the best structural solution. They were champions for the dominant narrative and had played a part in its development. The world of the Whitehall village spreads beyond the civil service to the media, and even to MPs, usually with little analysis or supporting evidence. After all, there are considerable advantages to civil servants in the DCLG in dealing with 100–150 large unitary authorities rather than the 350 or so widely varying selection that currently exist. We have heard civil servants say as much in unguarded moments, although none would ever publicly admit to this element of self-interest. Similarly, the disdain with which civil servants view councillors would be congruent with their lack of concern about a structural model that greatly reduces their number.

Equally, in local government, significant numbers of chief executives and council leaders saw opportunities in the acquisition of unitary status for their authorities: a bigger budget, a higher-profile leadership position, a larger chief executive salary. In several examples chief executives and council leaders worked together to persuade their councils to pass resolutions to reduce council size, when there was no requirement for them to do so (a further example of complicity in a narrative promoted by local as well as central actors). Thus, from 1992 onwards we had a local-government world in which the interests of civil servants corresponded with the interests of some (although by no means all) chief executives and council leaders.

The way forward

We are left with a dilemma. The existing local-government structure in England is a mess, full of inconsistencies and lacking any kind of coherent rationale. Diversity within the structure is not to be disparaged; indeed, it is to be welcomed if it reflects real differences of community identity. But diversity that has arisen from a series of ill-thought–through ad hoc initiatives is indeed a problem. In principle a root-and-branch reorganisation is required, which might (amongst other options) reintroduce the pre-1974 congruence between local councils and a sense of place (Jenkins 2004). But reorganisations always involve major upheavals, in which organisational energy is directed away from the key tasks of community governance and service delivery into fighting proposals for change and later, if change has been imposed, in implementing the new arrangements.

There are many more urgent challenges facing local government, in breaking free from the shackles of 40 years of oppressive centralisation, in particular the introduction of a stronger constitutional (or quasi-constitutional) status, a much more flexible system of local-government finance and a reallocation of service responsibilities on the subsidiarity principle. Therefore, one option is to put local-government reorganisation on the back burner, until these other more important issues have been dealt with.

Before the Scottish referendum in October 2014 we would have favoured this option. But from the panic that developed in the corridors of Westminster during the run-up to the referendum, when a vote for independence began to look like a real possibility, there emerged an unexpected and potentially beneficial spin-off for local government in England. As well as the promise of increased powers for the Scottish Parliament, and the Welsh and Northern Ireland Assemblies, all the major parties made a commitment to devolution within England. There was little detail about what form such devolution might take in any of the pre-2015 election party manifestos. But the commitment cannot easily be withdrawn or disregarded (or at least we hope not). English devolution would necessarily involve an examination of various local-government structures, which could put the idea into practice, as well as dealing with its constitutional and financial implications, and changes in the distribution of central and local functional responsibilities that would be required. Local-government reorganisation is back on the policy agenda, an observation confirmed by the 'Northern Powerhouse' initiative announced in November 2014. This policy initiative has since gone through a number of different stages (see Chapter 9), and is currently dominating the pages of the local-government journals. In this chapter we focus on the longer-term structural implications of the various varieties of 'combined authority' that are emerging

The issue of what form devolution should take is highly complex, and not to be taken lightly. The main problem is that, setting aside the debate about the need for an English parliament, there are (at least) three other territorial criteria on which English devolution could be organised, all of which have major deficiencies, as well as attractions: the provincial region, the city region, and the city.

If one of the government's aims in English devolution is to establish devolved units of equivalent size to Scotland (population 5 million) and Wales (population 3 million), then the provincial region option has much to recommend it. If the current regions (and the Greater London Authority) were to be retained, there would be nine devolved units, with an average population size of 6.5 million, broadly similar in size to Scotland and Wales.

The benefits of consistency of size in this option are, however, counteracted by the fact that provincial regions (with one or two exceptions) do not reflect a sense of local identity that begins to match that enjoyed by Scotland and Wales. The north-east, where the sense of regional identity is probably at its strongest, chose by a large margin not to take advantage of the opportunity for elected regional government in a referendum of 2004. Among the other provincial regions, while there are one or two with a degree of popular identity (for example, pre-1974 Yorkshire and the north-west), others have little. To create powerful devolved units that had little meaning for their inhabitants would be hard to justify. 'Home rule for the East Midlands' does not sound a plausible slogan! Nor would a Southern Region with powers that approached those enjoyed by Scotland be credible. There would also be the potential dangers of functions being taken from existing local authorities and allocated to these regional bodies. Scottish local authorities do not appear to have benefited from the existence of a Scottish parliament.

City regions, too, have a plausible basis for devolved units, but also major shortcomings. There is already one such city region in existence: the GLA, widely accepted since its creation in 2000 as a viable entity. Its capacity to deal with the interrelated challenges of transportation, infrastructure, and economic development and other functions would be just as relevant in the six metropolitan counties that were established in 1974. There are several other likely candidates: Greater Bristol, Nottingham, and Leicester, the Potteries and the Southampton/Portsmouth conurbation, which would all benefit from the ability to tackle such challenges in a strategic and coherent way. And if a key aim is to overcome the domination of (greater) London then this option has much to recommend it.

However, this option has two major drawbacks. First, what do you do with the substantial areas of England that do not fall within the ambit of a city region? It would be possible to designate rural regions in the spaces that were left, but they would not have any meaningful local identity. Or would we be dealing with a number of East Midlands counterparts, writ small? What would be likely to be involved would be an unconvincing set of amalgamations of counties (for example, Cumbria, Northumberland, and Durham in northern England).

Second, there's the question of where it would leave the 'big cities' that form the focal points of the city regions such as Manchester and Birmingham? It is hard to imagine a scenario where they would be abolished. But, as in 1974, their current range of responsibilities (and status) would necessarily be diminished. The government would have to consider the prospect of a re-instatement of the two-tier government in metropolitan areas, which would challenge its unitary predispositions.

In these circumstances, George Osborne's decision to devolve powers first to a Greater Manchester combined authority, headed by a directly elected mayor, and later to a range of other metropolitan (and non-metropolitan areas) is a worrying distraction (see below).

The third option would be to accelerate the drift to large unitary authorities, which has been the de facto policy of successive governments since 1986. This option would have the advantage of being relatively easy to implement; all the remaining counties that escaped the unitary solutions of the Banham Commission and the 2006–2008 process could now become unitary authorities. It would also retain the big cities as a primary focus for devolution, which reflects current government preferences. But there is little else that can be said in positive terms for this option. It would mean that any city regional governmental initiatives (for which there is undoubtedly a strong case) would have to be operated through joint machinery, which does not have a good track record in effectiveness or accountability. In the shires it would further distance local democracy from those settlements with which people most strongly identify (for example, Sevenoaks, Maidstone, and Canterbury in Kent) and result in some huge unitary counties, such as Essex, Hampshire and Kent itself, which has a larger population than several states in the USA!

It would be well nigh impossible to justify this outcome within a devolutionary agenda. The inconsistency between devolution as applied to Scotland and Wales and the use of the same concept applied to Wiltshire, Shropshire, or Gloucestershire would be transparent. There would in England be from 100 to 150 devolved units, with an average population of about 500,000. But how easy it would be, in these circumstances, for a government to argue that devolution had actually been achieved?

It is clear from the above discussion that there are no easy answers to the 'devolution within England' question. Devolution covers a much wider range of issues than territorial structure, in particular the constitutional and financial questions discussed in Chapters 5 and 6. But the current structure embraces a mass of inconsistencies, which it would be difficult to avoid addressing in any serious examination of devolutionary options, which would necessarily consider these questions. There is little value in structural reorganisation for its own sake. If structural change is to be set in motion, it must be fully integrated into or follow from a wide-ranging review that incorporates consideration of the role and purpose of local government, and the associated constitutional and financial issues. Without this context there would be real danger that it would provide a further distraction, and result in yet another unsatisfactory outcome. Considering the present haphazard way devolution is progressing under the 2015 Conservative government, it would be counter-productive at present to set in motion a structural reorganisation. Such a review and reorganisation is undoubtedly needed, but only after the more fundamental constitutional and financial issues have been addressed and recommendations agreed that would reverse the trend of centralisation that has gathered momentum throughout the past 35 years.

9

THE DEVOLUTION AGENDA

Throughout 2015 and 2016, the pages of the local-government press were dominated by news items and articles about (so-called) devolution, a policy initiative that raises important questions about the future of central–local relations. This chapter explores the development of this policy agenda – an often opaque process – and links it to the broader issues of the constitutional status, financing, territorial structures, and the political organisation of local government. We consider first the different stages of its development, from a metropolitan-region basis and then widening to later embrace non-metropolitan areas and (later still) to opportunities for a reorganisation involving a move to unitary authorities in two-tier areas. The motivation for the initiative and its longer-term objectives, so far as they can be identified, are next examined, followed by consideration of the extent to which what is happening can be seen as genuine devolution. The response of the world of local government, both collectively through the Local Government Association (LGA) and by individual local authorities, is examined. Finally, we identify various scenarios on how the initiative might further develop after the post-Brexit resignation of David Cameron as prime minister in June 2016, his subsequent replacement by Theresa May, and the other ministerial changes that followed, in particular the removal of George Osborne, the principal ministerial proponent of the Combined Authorities initiative, as chancellor of the exchequer.

The three phases of the process

In the aftermath of the September 2014 Scottish referendum result there was an all-party agreement to bring forward a devolution agenda, although without clarity as to what was meant by the term, not just for Scotland, to which further devolved powers had been promised in the run-up to the referendum, but also for Wales and Northern Ireland, and within England itself. The idea of an English Parliament was one element of this agenda. There was an awareness that it would be inconsistent if devolution measures were limited to the other three countries in the UK, whose populations ranged between 1.5 and 5 million, if England, with a population of approximately 60 million, were not included.

The first sign of what the government's concept of devolution might look like emerged before the Scottish referendum in June 2014, when Chancellor of the Exchequer George Osborne gave a speech in Manchester in which he introduced the idea of a 'Northern Powerhouse' in the following terms:

> The cities of the north are individually strong, but collectively not strong enough ... So the powerhouse of London dominates more and more. And that's not healthy for our economy. It's not good for our country. We need a Northern Powerhouse too. Not one city, but a collection of northern cities – sufficiently close to each other that combined they can take on the world.

In the months that followed, it was revealed that discussions were taking place between the chancellor, and the leaders and chief executives of the ten metropolitan district councils within the Greater Manchester area, that between 1974 and its abolition in 1986 had operated as a metropolitan county council and that had later acted collectively as the Association of Greater Manchester Authorities (AGMA). It later transpired, in the proposals that emerged in other areas, that what was involved was not a combination of the northern cities, but rather a series of separate initiatives.

The next section speculates on the reasons why the government might have embarked in this particular way on a project for devolution within England. We point out key features in its gestation. First, it was the chancellor himself who launched the project, rather than Eric Pickles, the secretary of state for Communities and Local Government (CLG). Osborne set a direction in which the Treasury continued to be the dominant mover and shaker, despite its limited understanding of the workings of local government beyond issues of finance, with the Department for Communities and Local Government (DCLG) playing a very limited role. Second, there was a general election due in May 2015, in which the Conservatives needed to do better in the northern metropolitan areas than they had in 2010 if they were to win an overall majority of seats in the House of Commons. Third, although the focus in the chancellor's statement was on cities, it soon became clear that the units for devolution would be city regions (and in particular the six former metropolitan counties) rather than cities such as Manchester, Liverpool, and Leeds. And, finally, George Osborne's own constituency, Tatton in north Cheshire, was on the edge of Greater Manchester. He was also known to regard the Labour leader of Manchester City Council, Richard Leese, and its chief executive, Howard Bernstein, as people with whom he could work with.

The first devolution deal was signed in Manchester in November 2014, establishing a Greater Manchester Combined Authority (GMCA) consisting of the ten leaders of the districts in the area. It was basically a continuation of AGMA that had proved more effective than any of the other successor arrangements in the six metropolitan areas in managing county-wide services such as public transport, waste disposal, and (until the introduction of police commissioners) the police service. But there was a new element in the political format of the combined authority, which the government insisted on as a condition for it to transfer to GMCA the full range of devolutionary responsibilities it was offering – there should be a directly-elected mayor to lead the combined authority when it was established in 2017. There had been little previous enthusiasm for such mayors in the city region; only Salford amongst the ten districts had one, and a 2011 referendum in Manchester had decisively rejected the idea. But unlike their metropolitan counterparts elsewhere (at least at first), this was a price the Greater Manchester authorities were prepared to pay to enjoy the fruits of devolution. The main responsibilities which were to be devolved were economic development (including business and employment support), substantial aspects of public transport policy and management, further education, and health and social care.

Similar deals followed, although there was some variation in the range of responsibilities devolved depending on the preparedness of the local authorities to accept the imposition of a directly elected mayor. The Sheffield City Region (previously South Yorkshire MCC) was the next to agree a deal, which may have had something to do with the fact that the constituency of the deputy prime minister, Nick Clegg, was in South Sheffield. By the spring of 2016 all the provincial metropolitan areas had agreed deals, with the exception of West Yorkshire, which was still in the process of negotiation. The five authorities on Teesside (the Tees Valley CA) had also done so. But with the exception of Tees Valley and Greater Manchester, the process of reaching agreement had been more problematical. Gateshead opted out of the North East CA (which also includes Northumberland and Durham) leaving a hole in its centre. Chesterfield has opted to join the South Yorkshire CA rather than an authority based on Derbyshire and Nottinghamshire, much to the annoyance of the latter. The imposition of a directly elected mayor has been resisted everywhere, particularly strongly on Merseyside and in the West Midlands, but eventually grudgingly accepted.

While the metropolitan deals were still being negotiated in the spring of 2015, the initiative entered a second phase where any grouping of authorities or, in Cornwall, a single authority, could make a bid to become a combined authority. The adoption of a directly elected mayor still appeared to be a condition for a successful bid, although several groups of authorities put in a bid without having agreed amongst themselves to accept this condition. The nature of the initiative had drifted from one that was city region-based to one that (apparently) anyone could join, as long as they were prepared to play by the rules. The rules remained far from clear, although there were some indications that less importance was being given to elected mayors in the county areas. The invitation soon generated a strange mix of bids, including one from the whole of East Anglia (embracing 22 local authorities, including three counties), Greater Lincolnshire (which doesn't incorporate anything north of the Humber), Cornwall (on its own, and without being required to have a directly elected mayor), and West of England (what used to be Avon County Council).

Then, in February 2016, as the Cities and Local Government Devolution Bill, which was to be the legislative basis of the devolution process, was being discussed in the House of Lords, the initiative moved into a third phase, with the announcement that the government were now offering three devolutionary options: first, a deal with a directly elected mayor; second, a deal involving a move to unitary authorities with no directly elected mayor; or, third, no deal. What had started as a relatively circumscribed 'Northern Powerhouse' initiative was now turning into a free-for-all, with devolution in those non-metropolitan areas still operating under a two-tier system being offered as an incentive to secure their agreement to a unitary system of local government. It was not long before attempts were made to seize this unexpected opportunity, although none of them has yet been able to secure agreement between the county and districts involved.

First came the five districts of Oxfordshire, with a proposal, backed by the county's four MPs (including David Cameron), to dispense with the county council and operate with five unitary district-based authorities, which would then collaborate with Cotswolds District Council (Gloucestershire) and South Northamptonshire District Council in a Combined Authority. Then it was the turn of the Northamptonshire districts, again spurred on by the county's MPs, to propose a similar scheme that would do away with the county. Similar initiatives followed, including a 'breakaway' proposal from five districts in East Kent. In each case, the county criticised the proposal, arguing that a unitary county would be a better option. It was all predictable, evoking memories of the county–district sparring inspired by the appointment of the Banham Commission in 1991 and the Labour government's botched reorganisation of 2006–2008 (see Chisholm and Leach 2008). The idea of devolution had apparently almost disappeared, to be replaced by the distractions of a further reorganisation.

The present state-of-play is that there are several proposals still being negotiated – a total of 34 proposals in all have been received. But there is a sense of hiatus. The new secretary of state for Communities and Local Government, Sajid Javid, has stated that devolution will go ahead. But the driving forces behind the initiative – George Osborne, and (to a less extent) Greg Clark – are no longer involved, and it is unlikely that their replacements will have the same level of commitment to the project. Preparations for the Brexit negotiations are going to take up vast amounts of civil servants' time over the next 12 months or so, with other time-consuming activities, such as the negotiation of devolution deals, reducing greatly in priority, or perhaps even being put on hold.

Objectives and motives of the centre

Can the devolution process be seen as a prime example of what Chares Lindblom (1965) called 'disjointed incrementalism', which views most governmental policy-making as proceeding not as a rational long-term strategy, but rather through the modification of existing policy in a sequence of small sideways steps? Or is it better viewed as a devious tacit strategy, in which the 'Northern Powerhouse' was promoted as the first stage of a process that would eventually lead to a central–local settlement radically different from the current arrangements?

The way in which the initiative developed in three different but related stages suggests an incremental explanation. George Osborne had previously shown no particular interest in local government, although in his last year of office he had become interested in the restoration of the business rate as a means of giving local authorities adequate financial resources to cover their responsibilities, an idea soon shown to be both unlikely to achieve this aim, and also to involve unanticipated complexities (see Chapter 6). Indeed, few senior government figures, including successive chancellors over the past 50 years or so, have shown much interest in local government, except, notably, Michael Heseltine and John Prescott. The interest of chancellors, and the Treasury, has usually been limited to restricting the expenditure of local government, as part of a macro-economic strategy. The most likely explanation of George Osborne's first devolutionary moves is political opportunism. A general election was due within a year, and there was a political imperative to demonstrate some form of commitment to the big cities, particularly in the north of England, where the Conservatives struggled to win seats in the 2010 election – hence the Northern Powerhouse speech in June 2014. The chancellor's contacts with and good opinion of senior politicians and leaders in Greater Manchester, together with the impressive track record of these authorities of operating collectively, made this area the obvious choice for the development of a model that could then be applied in other city regions, at the same time as winning electoral support for the Conservatives.

Why would the chancellor want to impose a directly elected mayor as a condition for agreeing a deal? The coalition government (or at least the dominant party within it) had previously expressed enthusiasm for the idea, initiating in 2013 referenda in 10 cities on the adoption of a directly elected mayor. David Cameron talked enthusiastically about the prospect of 'a Boris in every major city' – a reference to the perceived success, at the time, of Boris Johnson, then in his second term as Mayor of London. But only one city – Bristol – voted in favour, although Doncaster voted to continue with a mayor, a surprising outcome given the controversy over previous holders of the office. It is likely that senior civil servants, too, especially in DCLG, would have been advocating directly elected mayors, a goal they have long desired. But Osborne would have known that in each of the city regions forming combined authorities, there was a strong probability of a Labour directly elected mayor, or, failing that, some kind of independent, who would break Labour's dominance. Maybe there was an instinctive and ill-considered belief in the virtues of one-person rule, preferably by someone with the perceived charisma of Boris Johnson, was what decided the chancellor to impose the condition.

But then, in the second stage, the devolution initiative mysteriously changed from one that is focused solely on the former metropolitan-county areas, plus Tees Valley, and became nation-wide in its scope, or at least an opportunity that any group of authorities anywhere can bid to become part of. In February 2016 the opportunity was widened to include groups of authorities in two-tier areas prepared to submit a proposal for unitary local government. Suspicions grew that such devolution was not simply short-term political opportunism inspired by an approaching election, but contained elements of a 'conspiracy' encompassing a more wide-ranging plan for restructuring local government.

Was there a 'hidden agenda' here? Behind the initial portrayal of the initiative as devolution to combined authorities, there could have been a long-term plan by the Conservative government (shared by Labour governments) to move to a simplified nation-wide system of local government involving large unitary authorities headed by directly elected mayors. In the metropolitan areas where combined authorities have already been established, or will be shortly, the new structures are perhaps envisaged as the first stage in a move to a unitary system in which the metropolitan districts (including big cities such as Manchester, Liverpool, and Birmingham) are later found to be 'surplus to requirements', given their increasingly limited range of responsibilities. In the non-metropolitan areas, the encouragement to explore unitary options would make it easier, in due course, to redefine the combined authorities as unitary authorities. The end-result for example for the Oxfordshire districts could be that in bidding for unitary status they may, if successful, be unwittingly sowing the seeds of their own demise!

Another possibility is that the change of direction in stage three was a piece of opportunism, this time by senior civil servants in DCLG. It is unlikely that George Osborne had much interest in local-government structure, or that he envisaged a move in this direction when he first announced the Northern Powerhouse initiative. But DCLG officials have a long-term enthusiasm for a uniform unitary system of local government, which they believe would make their administrative responsibilities for the sector much easier to manage. Incoming ministers are generally susceptible to the policy predispositions of the departments to which they are appointed. The Labour-initiated reorganisation of 2006–2008 was announced shortly after the appointment of a new minister, Ruth Kelly. Greg Clark had been appointed secretary of state for Communities and Local Government in

May 2010, and would have been subject to the same kind of pressure. That is the most likely explanation for the 'unitary' emphasis to the policy, introduced in stage three.

Little attention has been given to the long-term implications of this move, and the scope for the future unification of the Combined Authorities. There would be several difficult obstacles to be overcome. It is hardly likely that a Conservative (or indeed, any) government would consider abolishing the great city councils of Manchester, Liverpool, and Birmingham with their 150 years of history. But if the responsibility for adult social care were to be switched to the metropolitan combined authorities, which is highly likely, and if the devolution of health powers became the norm and local authorities were left with only a vestigial responsibility for primary and secondary education, then there would be little more for the once-great cities than a miscellaneous rag-bag of functional responsibilities. The government would be unlikely to abolish the 32 London boroughs (although there have been suggestions that it might merge them into five or six much larger units). If two-tier government remains entrenched in the capital, this would undermine the goal of a nationwide unitary system. It would highlight the anomaly that if two-tier local government were seen as appropriate for London, why should it not also be reintroduced in the provincial city regions, where the Combined Authorities now being established are in effect multipurpose joint boards, under the leadership of one directly elected individual: the directly elected mayor?

The most convincing explanation for the government's love affair with devolution is one that combines elements of incrementalism, and opportunism, underpinned by long-held civil service goals. The launch of the project has the feel of pre-election political opportunism. But the subsequent stages probably owe more to civil-service priorities than they do to strongly held political views. In particular, the move to unitary government in stage three of the process bears the hallmarks of a piece of civil-service opportunism. In our judgement, a crucial point about the current position of central government towards devolution is that it has attached two major strings, more like thick ropes. They are two goals long desired by central-government civil servants: local-government structural reorganisation and directly elected mayors. This position illustrates the institutional fallacy that is embedded in the culture of the civil service that problems can be resolved, and change brought about by structural change, without an adequate understanding of the roles of the institutions concerned.

Devolution? What devolution?

There has been some devolution of responsibilities from central government to a more local level, which in principle is to be welcomed. But devolution in the form it has been offered and widely accepted should be viewed with circumspection for several reasons. First, it comes with strings attached, notably 'structural reorganisation' and 'directly elected mayors', both of which involve real dangers to the long-term future of local government. Second, the devolution of service responsibilities has not been accompanied by fiscal devolution, which is an essential component of a viable system of genuinely local government. Third, most of the devolution that has taken place has been to local units far larger in area and population than almost all existing authorities. Fourth, the process is likely to involve the switch of responsibilities from districts up to combined authorities – the reverse of what is usually understood by devolution. Fifth, on the government's agenda is the devolution of a range of responsibilities that it is in its interests to devolve, and are likely to prove more of a problem than a benefit to the local authorities. Finally, there is an ill-thought-out challenge to the principles of local representative democracy, in that most of the devolution responsibilities are being placed in the hands of indirectly elected authorities, which are in essence multi-purpose joint boards – a structural device much criticised by both major parties ever since their introduction in the aftermath of the abolition in 1986 of the GLC and the six metropolitan counties. That these de facto joint boards are to be led by directly elected mayors is a small but totally inadequate gesture in the direction of local democracy and accountability.

We have already expressed our concern about the longer-term implications of the strings (or ropes) attached to devolution deals. We argue that there should be no doubt that the government is engaged in a project of major structural change of local government, first to get sub-regional or regional authorities through combined authorities, based on the faulty principle that bigger is better, and, second, to cut the number of elected councillors, and to reduce their role, by creating directly elected mayors based on the faulty principle of one-person rule. Its policy of devolving extended powers and functions to local authorities is a bribe to local government to do what central government wants, which would damage local government.

As noted in Chapter 6, the future of local-government finance is plagued with uncertainties. There are signs that central government wishes to reduce significantly the level of central grant over the 2015–2020 period. It has argued that this reduction could be compensated for by the return of business rates to local authorities, increases in council tax, specific grants, and other funding pots. But this list does not amount to a coherent strategy to change the way in which local government is financed, and takes no account of the need to include an equalisation mechanism, to compensate for the major differences in the resource base and needs faced by different authorities. Given that combined authorities are not local authorities as such, one assumes that for the present they will be funded by a series of specific grants from the centre, each earmarked to finance one of the transferred services. We do not yet know whether there will be any scope for combined authorities to switch resources between different devolved services? They may well feel under considerable pressure to do so, particularly if, as is proposed, health is one of the services concerned, as in Greater Manchester. One assumes that the transfer of heath responsibilities to a combined authority will be accompanied by a specific grant reflecting current allocations made to the National Health Service (NHS) in that particular area. In the not unlikely event of the budget allocated proving inadequate, the combined authority would be faced with the choice of finding top-up resources from somewhere, or dealing with a growing wave of public protest, or conceivably both!

The House of Commons Select Committee on Communities and Local Government report *Devolution: The Next Five Years and Beyond* emphasised its concerns about the lack of fiscal devolution to accompany the devolution of service responsibilities. The Committee chair Clive Betts said, 'There is an understanding that devolution can't just be about handing power down, it has to be about finance too. The two strands have to work hand in hand.' A witness from a Greater Manchester authority made the point more sharply: 'We have devolution powers with almost no devolution of borrowing power … it's utterly nonsensical.' The implication is clear: if the government is serious about devolution, it has to come up with a proposal for some form of fiscal devolution that would remove the financial restrictions on local-government expenditure that currently exist, and free up both combined authorities and local authorities generally to play the devolutionary role expected of them.

The units to which powers are being devolved (and in some cases moved upward from metropolitan districts or county councils) are all regional or subregional in scale, with populations in most cases well in excess of the largest present shire counties (for example, Kent, Essex, and Lancashire). The North-East Combined Authority covers the whole region (minus Tees Valley and Gateshead) and has a population approaching 2 million. The East Anglia

Combined Authority has a similar regional basis, and a population of approximately one and a half million. It introduces a third tier of local government – something of a problem for the unitary enthusiasts in DCLG! All the combined authorities based on the former metropolitan counties have populations of the same (or greater) size. They are very large local authorities by any standards. Devolution to regional or sub-regional amalgamations of this nature is different from devolution to the spatial units with which people most readily identify: cities, towns, and to, a lesser extent, counties. Over the last two decades, supporters of local democracy have framed the devolution debate with the principles of subsidiarity, namely that public responsibilities shall generally be exercised, in preference, by those authorities that are closest to the citizen (Article 4 (3) of the European Charter of Local Self-Government). These principles imply the desirability of 'double devolution': the devolution of powers and responsibilities from central government to local authorities, and then, where possible, further devolution from local authorities to town and parish councils or to local neighbourhood or ward councils set up by authorities themselves. What we have in the current devolution agenda is the antithesis of devolution, involving some transfer of responsibilities upward from local authorities to a non-elected Combined Authority, and in most cases to a directly elected mayor. Where this approach leaves town and parish councils is anyone's guess.

Combined Authorities and Metro Mayors have been allocated sweeping powers over a number of important functions, in a way bound to erode over time the discretion and independence of the individual local authorities represented on a Combined Authority. The functions appearing in current devolution deals include roads, transport, spatial planning, land disposal, housing investment, further education and skills, employment and business support, health and social care, and policing. It is acknowledged that some strategic elements of these functions, and the funding for them, are currently the responsibility of central government, but local authorities too have key responsibilities in most of these areas. Indeed, the Cities and Local Government Devolution Act 2016 Explanatory Note makes it clear that Combined Authorities will be 'receiving a number of new powers from local authorities' as well as devolved powers from government departments and agencies. If devolution in its current form gathers further momentum, and most of these services and functions end up with combined authorities (and if responsibility for education continues to move away from local authorities), then the historic cities such as Manchester and Liverpool may end up with sole responsibility for little more than libraries and leisure, trading standards, and consumer protection, local planning applications, and refuse collection. They would have a similar range of responsibilities to shire districts, such as East Lindsey, South Ribble, West Dorset, and North Warwickshire – a bizarre outcome indeed of so-called devolution!

Some of the functions currently being proposed for devolution are ones where there is more advantage to central government in divesting itself of them than to local authorities in acquiring them. For example, it is becoming clear that the government has a long-term aim of devolving much of the social security and benefits budget to local government, without the enhanced resources (and flexibility in deploying them) that would avoid the need for restrictive rationing. Hardship payments have already been transferred. The Independent Living Fund has been closed, and responsibility passed to local government, with no ring-fenced resources. More recently, it has emerged that the government intends to transfer the huge Attendance Allowance budget to local authorities. This move is highly convenient for the centre, but does local government really wish to become the gate-keeper and rationer-in-chief of such benefits at a time of continuing austerity?

The most powerful criticism of devolution in its current form is that it undermines the principles on which local democracy is based. It does not involve the transfer of powers to an elected local authority, but rather to a multi-purpose joint board, headed by an elected mayor. There is a worrying undemocratic flaw in devolving so much responsibility to an unelected authority. In the Greater Manchester Combined Authority the membership (with the exception of the mayor) consists of the leaders of the ten metropolitan boroughs within the area. They have not been elected to the Combined Authority; they have in effect been appointed by the councils that they lead. They are delegates, and in as far as combined authorities can be seen as democratic, it can only be as an example of 'delegate democracy' (see Gyford et al 1989, pp342–8). But delegate democracy requires those delegated to be mandated by the body they represent, and to adhere to that mandate in any debate and voting that takes place. It also requires the delegate to 'report back' to the parent body on the outcomes of these debates and votes. In theory these processes could take place, but in reality they rarely do. This conclusion was drawn from the research on the behaviour of the joint boards (and in Greater Manchester, the overarching Association of Greater Manchester Authorities) following the abolition in 1986 of the six metropolitan county councils (Leach et al 1992). Little mandating or reporting back took place. The joint boards invariably operated in a detached way from the local authorities represented on them, and AGMA was run by an equally detached coterie of council leaders. Such behaviour is typical of joint boards throughout history, which is one of the reasons all parties (including the Conservatives), have been so critical of them in the 1997–2010 period. Thus, unless the various combined authorities manage to break with the behaviour patterns of their predecessors (which is possible but highly unlikely) there will be a major democratic deficit in the way that they operate.

There is a further issue of democratic concern. No manifestos will be available from the various political parties, with details of what their policies would be if they became the dominant force on a combined authority. There would be no point, because, in the absence of elections, they would serve no purpose. The mayoral candidates will have personal manifestos of some description. But the extent to which they will be in a position to implement them will depend on the constitutional powers allocated to them (which will be decided in advance of their election and may be expected to tilt the balance of power towards the local-authority members, rather than the mayor), and their ability to impose their will on a group of experienced (and suspicious) council leaders. Whatever the outcome, the possibility of any meaningful input from the citizens of the areas covered by the combined authorities, beyond the vote cast at the mayoral election, is remote. This feature constitutes a second serious democratic flaw in the devolution arrangements.

The arrangements for combined authorities weaken local democracy in another way. The proposals represent a major extension of the concept of 'super majorities', with the combined authorities able to defeat a proposal by the mayor, but only if they gain a two-thirds majority. This provision departs from the established and well-understood principle of majority voting, and replaces it with the more democratically-opaque principle of a specified level of the majority required.

The response of local authorities to devolution

It was perhaps not surprising that the Greater Manchester authorities, having been singled out by the second most important minister in the government as an example of good practice, should have enthusiastically embraced the devolutionary offer made to them, despite their reservations about the imposition of a directly elected mayor. That set a precedent amongst the other metropolitan areas, who did not want to miss out on a rare offer from the government of enhanced powers, particularly when Greater Manchester was enthusiastically signing up to the project. There have been more difficulties in reaching agreement in the other areas, particularly over the unpopular requirement for a directly elected mayor, but they have all agreed deals, or are close to doing so. In noting the comments of the leaders of the metropolitan districts in the pages of the *Municipal Journal*, there is a strong sense of 'if this is the only game in town, we'll go along with it'. This devolution proposal was the first positive initiative (despite the strings attached) from central government since 2010. Although the local authorities might have done well to pay more attention to the longer-term implications of the journey they were embarking on, their positive, if sometimes qualified, response was understandable.

Less appropriate, although totally predictable, was the response to the third phase of the devolution initiative – the opportunity in the shires for groups of authorities to achieve a devolution deal in return for a commitment to moving to a unitary system of local government. If ever there was a move certain to set counties against districts, it was this. Groups of districts submitted proposals arguing for the abolition of counties, which were then refuted by counties, or vice versa.

In these circumstances, conspiracy theories move back on the agenda. The government, and the civil servants who advise it, must have known, from previous experience that this kind of county-district conflict would be the consequence. Was it a deliberate attempt to 'divide and rule', and, if so, how could that have been justified, in the context of what appeared to have been an attempt to work with groups of local authorities to establish cooperative arrangements between central and local government through mutually agreed devolution deals? The LGA, which could have condemned the divide-and-rule implications of phase 3 remained silent, another example of the ineffectiveness of this organisation in identifying and acting on what is in the best interests of local government as a whole.

Future developments

As of August 2016, the future of the government's devolution initiative was still uncertain. Assurances about its continuation have been given by the new Communities and Local Government Secretary of State Sajid Javid, but not by Phillip Hammond, the new chancellor of the exchequer. Over the next couple of years, the government has bigger issues to deal with, in particular negotiating the exit from Europe and dealing with a widely forecast recession. Civil servants in DCLG are likely to continue to push hard for the devolution agenda, in particular the 'unitary authorities' element. Indeed, there was a significant development in November 2016, when in a speech to the County Councils Network conference, Sajid Javid gave a ringing endorsement to unitary local government, telling delegates that he would like to see unitary councils of populations from 300,000 to 500,000 established across the country. The DCLG line appears to have been accepted yet again by a new minister with little knowledge or experience of local government, and the democratically-indefensible prospect of a local-government structure comprising 150 very large unitary authorities is back on the agenda.

One possibility is that devolution drifts into a low-priority zone, permitted to continue in combined authorities that have already been established, or are well on the way to establishment. Its scope would not be widened and its operation would become increasingly routinised. However if, as suggested above, there is a hidden agenda within the DCLG working towards a nationwide system of large unitary authorities, then we might expect to see phase 3 of the agenda given prominence, a development for which evidence is beginning to emerge as 2016 draws to a close. This approach may in due course result in the Government imposing unitary 'solutions' on groups of counties and districts unable or unwilling to reach agreement, as it did in 2008, and regardless of the disruption caused by such imposed changes. How this outcome would facilitate 'devolution', beyond the limited proposed allocation of responsibilities and resources to the new unitaries, is far from clear.

On balance, should devolution, in its current form, be seen as a welcome move in the direction of strengthening the position of local government, in the way that we have advocated? Can it be seen as a positive response to the concerns we have expressed about current shortcomings in the constitutional and financial status of local government, and its territorial and political management? The answer to both questions is that it cannot. The initiative is a patchwork quilt, which gives the impression of having been stitched up as it has gone along. There may be an element of a hidden agenda – large unitary authorities – contained within it, but, if so, the inconsistencies within the agenda have not been recognised. It fails to address the key constitutional issues facing the central–local government relationship; indeed, it provides a further example of the centre providing a 'strings attached' opportunity on a 'take it or leave it' basis, which, understandably but unwisely, many authorities have taken. It fails to link the devolution of responsibilities with fiscal devolution, a topic that seems to have no place on the government's agenda, but is an essential feature of any move to strengthen local government as a democratic, genuinely governmental, institution. It imposes a form of political management (elected mayors), whose effectiveness is unproven, and that is unpopular with local populations and their elected councillors alike. It will create an even more incoherent territorial structure of local government, a mix of unitary authorities, two-tier government, and combined authorities with opaque accountability mechanisms, and with local-authority populations varying from 38,000 (unitary Rutland) to more than 2 million (the East Anglia Combined Authority).

By far the most worrying aspect of the current initiative is that it will come to be seen as 'English Devolution', the government's response to the all-party pledge made in the aftermath of the Scottish referendum to introduce devolutionary measures in all the constituent countries of the UK, and within England – by far the largest country of the four. What we are seeing emerge in no way constitutes a serious, considered response to the complex challenges of devolution within England. Rather, it is a messy series of ill-considered measures aimed at giving the impression that the Government wishes to change the central–local power balance in favour of the local. All of the evidence and arguments set out in this chapter, together with other government policies, such as an accelerated move to academies in education, suggest otherwise. The march of centralisation continues.

10

REFLECTIONS AND CONCLUSIONS

From 2010, and until the emergence onto the policy agenda in 2014 of English devolution, discussions about the future of the public sector and of local government within it were invariably focused on the challenges posed by 'austerity', the coalition government's response to the national (and, indeed, global) financial crisis engendered by the collapse of the banking system in 2008–2009. Whether 'austerity' was the most appropriate response has increasingly come to be challenged (see Jones 2014 and others), but it provided a convenient rationale for a range of contentious fiscal measures by the coalition, including a public-sector pay freeze, reductions in the level of grant paid by central government to local authorities, and severe constraints on their spending levels. These measures were underpinned by a series of ideological beliefs, including the need to 'roll back' (or shrink) the state (including the welfare budget), and the commitment, wherever possible, to the privatisation of public services (see Meek 2014).

In these circumstances, the concerns we have expressed throughout this book about the inexorable decline in the powers and status of local government since the early 1980s (and particularly since 2010) may seem of little importance. The government's dominant perspective on local government has been an economic one, premised on its perceived need to control the total level of public expenditure, a view open to challenge, if one distinguishes between the level of central-government grant and the finance raised by local authorities themselves through council tax and charges (see

Chapter 6). Those writing about the detrimental impact of the cuts in the welfare budget on the lives of those reliant on state benefits, or in low-paid or insecure work (see O'Hara 2014; Toynbee and Walker 2014), have drawn attention to the ways in which local authorities have contributed further to the problems of these groups, such as the withdrawal of funding from advice centres and of council-tax-relief provisions. Typically, however, the authors have acknowledged that councils have often had little choice, given the scale of the cuts they have been required to make, and the range of statutory services they have had to safeguard in doing so.

The growing intensity of the financial crisis facing local authorities that had become apparent by the end of 2016, particularly in the larger cities, was made clear by Birmingham's chief executive Mark Rogers in an interview in *The Guardian* (13 December). He warned that there would be cata-strophic consequences for some in the city because years of cuts had forced the council to slash funding for key services for the most vulnerable. As a result of six years of austerity, 'the youth service had all but gone, home-lessness prevention services had been cut by so much that rough sleeping had quadrupled, and far fewer elderly people were eligible for care at home'. Children's centres designed to serve the city's most deprived com-munities had been dismantled, so that it was now only the 'super-deprived' who were being helped. 'The big disaster that is coming is if the govern-ment doesn't do anything about social care,' he added, a view echoed in authorities with this responsibility throughout the country. In Walsall there it is feared that all branch libraries will have to close next year, leaving a library service consisting of one central library only on a borough with a population approaching 300,000. And there is more to come. By 2020, Birmingham will have been required to make UK£800 million worth of cuts over a ten-year period. Could these devastating outcomes ever have been envisaged prior to 2010?

But there is a second, crucially important, dimension to the role of local government, which has been constantly overlooked ever since the early 1980s (and increasingly so since 2010), namely that of its democratic vitality and viability. The past 40 years have seen a constant and cumulative erosion of its powers and responsibilities, reflecting the ever-increasing centralisation in the central–local relationship. There is now a palpable democratic deficit in the government of England, of which the current marginalised state of local government is the most worrying manifestation. Its capacity for com-munity governance – that is, the scope for making local choices about local issues and to resource them – has been undermined ever since the Thatcher years (see Jenkins 1994), but has become particularly apparent since the advent of the coalition government, and looks set to continue, unless the devolution agenda can be taken forward on a wide-ranging basis following the 2015 election.

In the inter-war years of austerity and economic downturn local authorities, if they were so minded, could and did make a significant contribution to the relief of poverty and deprivation (see Brockway 1949; and, on Poplarism, Branson 1979). They were able to do so because they had much more financial flexibility than is currently the case, with the rates contributing a much greater proportion of council income than council tax does now, and with no central-government restrictions on the level at which the rates were set. These kinds of choices in response to local deprivation are hardly possible at present, because of the restrictions placed on local-authority expenditure (see Chapter 6). Reintroducing a significant level of budgetary flexibility would make a big difference to the capacity of local authorities to make real choices at a local level, including measures to ameliorate poverty by the restoration of council-tax relief, the support of welfare-rights centres, emergency payments, and other council services that have suffered from the cuts. It would also enable them to operate as genuine governmental institutions, responding to the unique combinations of social, economic, and environmental challenges in their areas in an integrated and locally sensitive fashion, rather than (as at present) as underfunded agencies for the provision (or commissioning) of increasingly centrally specified services. Liberating changes in local-government financial arrangements are by no means a sufficient condition for the achievement of this kind of capacity, but they are an essential first step. They would strengthen the position of local government in the 'unitary state' of our unwritten constitution, and so lead to an enhanced sense of democratic viability and vitality within it.

But for this desirable outcome to take place, there would, as noted in the Introduction, have to be profound changes in the way in which local government was perceived, valued, and dealt with by the centre. In a recent article, Jones and Stewart (2016, p16) identified a series of failings of the British system of government, which have arisen because of 'excessive and growing centralisation and inadequate and confused accountability'. These defects, all of which have been illustrated at various times throughout the book, are listed below:

• the excessive prescription by central-government departments, remote from the problems faced by citizens and the challenges of service provision in a local context, reflecting their failure to understand the requirements of governing in a complex and multi-level system of government;

- the expression of that prescription in over-detailed primary legislation and ever-increasing secondary legislation, which curtail innovation and initiative at the local level by those who have to carry out the requirements of the legislation, but have a better understanding of what is required than those drafting it;
- the growth in the scope of central government, leading to dis-economies of scale, and consequent weaknesses of communication between departments, within departments, and between departments and arms-length delivery agencies;
- the dominance of the fallacy that problems can be solved by structural change, which leads to institutional instability, as each change creates its own problems for those who work in the organisations concerned (NHS or local government), or receive services from them;
- the fragmentation of the system of government in localities, as public-sector agencies and QUANGOS multiply, and are often then amended, creating a complex and little understood system of local governance;
- the neglect of the growing problems of accountability, as agencies are established at local level with no clear lines of accountability beyond a remote, theoretical link to central government;
- the growth of procedures and plans laid down by central government that involve significant use of resources (including specific grants), and that typically distract attention from the problems and issues faced by those working at the local level.

They are all symptoms of a failing system of government. Underlying these symptoms is the distorted relationship between central government and those who work in local authorities and other local agencies, where it has so often proved difficult to achieve mutual understanding. There has also been neglect by the centre of the resources, experience, and initiative that lies in the complex network of governance at the local level. The centralist perspective assumes (wrongly) that effective government depends entirely upon central government, which necessitates detailed control by the centre for fear that local authorities (and other local bodies) charged with local responsibilities will undermine central policy. There is a familiar 'what if?' refrain. What if local authorities were allowed freedom to develop policy in areas where the centre has an interest? The assumption is that the centre better understands local needs than those who have to deal with them in practice.

It follows that whatever statutory or quasi-constitutional changes were to be introduced that might strengthen local government, there would remain the problem of the arrogant and dismissive attitude to local government that dominates Whitehall and Westminster. The centralist culture is expressed in a series of assumptions, widely held by civil servants, and often also by ministers and MPs. It is sustained and reinforced in the discourse of the linked villages of Whitehall and Westminster. This assumptive world includes, amongst others, the following constituents, all unsupported by evidence:

- the 'low calibre' of councillors;
- the more limited abilities of local-authority staff, compared with the civil service;
- the tendency of members of the public with problems to seek out MPs rather than local councillors;
- the view that a national mandate should always prevail over a local mandate;
- the perception of the 'postcode lottery' as a problem, rather than the expression of local choice;
- the infallibility of inspectors and inspections, when compared with the views of those inspected;
- the inefficiency of local authorities, compared with central government.

Underlying all of these assumptions is an elite contempt for the world of local government, and the councillors and officers within it. Unless the existence of these misconceptions are acknowledged within the centre, and some way is found of stimulating cultural change there, then the problems will return, whatever redistribution of responsibilities is introduced. Changing culture is a more difficult, but ultimately a more effective way of changing behaviour and performance, as many chief executives can confirm from their own experience.

A case could be made that the change of culture we are advocating is already beginning to take place, given the commitment (in principle) of all the major parties to English devolution, and the measures already introduced since George Osborne's 2014 'Northern Powerhouse' speech to put this principle into operation, through the Combined Authorities initiative. But, as we saw in Chapter 9, several features of this initiative do not support the idea that a change of this nature is really taking place. So far, devolution has been made conditional (in most cases) on the local authorities accepting a political structure based on an elected mayor, a move that is opposed by most councils and has been rejected in referenda in most of the major cities.

There has been no move to link the devolution of service responsibilities in the Combined Authorities to fiscal devolution, a concern expressed in the House of Commons Select Committee Report on Devolution (2016). And an extension of this agenda to include a further attempt to persuade local authorities outside the metropolitan areas to introduce unitary systems of local government has (yet again) set counties against districts in many parts of the country. The initiative smacks of ad hoc pre-election political opportunism rather than a genuine reassessment of the state of central–local relations by the centre, and does not begin to address the underlying problems we have identified.

The Combined Authorities initiative, despite its transfer of selected responsibilities from the centre to selected collectives of local authorities, is no substitute for a comprehensive reassessment of central–local relations and in particular government structure. In recent issues of the *Municipal Journal*, there have been calls for a Royal Commission to be established to deal with the increasingly chaotic structure that is emerging. Combined Authorities are not an adequate response to the complexities of the devolution agenda, and the big choices encompassed within it. It would be a tragedy for English local government if this once-in-a-generation opportunity were not to be grasped. There is a legacy of 40 years of piecemeal but cumulative marginalisation of local government that urgently needs to be addressed, if we are to recreate a democratic system with a proper balance between the centre and the localities.

In principle, an exercise involving the objectivity and thoroughness typically associated with Royal Commissions is the kind of approach that is needed to deal with current constitutional financial and structural mess in which local government finds itself. However, there are drawbacks to Royal Commissions, of which the most important is the time they take to report, and then for their recommendations to be considered and (partly or wholly) implemented. Five years from start to finish would be a conservative estimate. Local government cannot afford a further five years in limbo, with the probability of further austerity-fuelled resource cutbacks, and the opportunity of genuine devolution inspired by the 2014 Scottish independence referendum result gradually fading into the background.

Our proposal would be for a process to be set in motion that was in effect a speeded-up version of a Royal Commission, with the same degree of objectivity and commitment to evidence-based recommendations, but working to a brief that requires it to report within a year. A task force would perhaps be the most relevant designation for such a body, a term that emphasises the urgency of its remit. Its brief should cover constitutional and financial issues and political and electoral arrangements, but not issues of territorial structure that would make its job unmanageable. Such issues would need to be subjected to the same rigorous evidence-based process, as a 'second stage' to be dealt with after the more fundamental constitutional and financial issues had been dealt with and a strengthened system of local government re-established. It would be appropriate for the task force to draw on the work of the various independent Committees of Inquiry or Commissions that have operated over the past 40 years: Layfield, certainly, Widdicombe, and (with more reservations) Banham. Its report should be considered by the Joint Committee of the House of Commons and House of Lords, which was one of our key constitutional proposals set out in Chapter 5.

Changes are needed to revitalise local government, and reverse the trend of centralisation that has become increasingly dominant since the 1980s. Set out below is a summary of the key proposals we have argued are needed (in Chapters 5–8). They do not constitute a blueprint, which would be beyond the scope of a book of this nature, but should be seen as a road map, which would help redress a central–local imbalance in a way that is long overdue.

Constitutional change

- The position of local government in a unitary state should be protected by a quasi-constitutional statute, drawn up by an independent task force, working to a limited time scale.
- To ensure that the statute is respected, there should be established a unit at the heart of central government, possibly within the cabinet office, with the responsibility of monitoring whether the principles set out in the statute were being embedded in government policies, and overseeing whether action taken by individual departments was consistent with them.
- There should also be established a joint committee of both houses of Parliament to monitor the application of the agreed principles, and on specific proposals, reporting annually to Parliament.

- The statute should contain the following principal elements (for a fuller list, see Chapter 5):

  o   a statement that the primary role of local government exercised by local councils is the government of local communities, ensuring their well-being;

  o   a statement that local government should be provided with adequate powers and resources to carry out this primary role, acting under its own responsibility;

  o   a statement that action by central government in local affairs is justified only when there is a clear national interest involved;

  o   a statement that the primary accountability of local authorities is to local residents;

  o   the basic duties and powers of local authorities should be protected by statute;

  o   the general power of competence should be confirmed, enabling local authorities to take any action that would benefit their communities that were not within the responsibilities of other public agencies;

  o   public responsibilities should be exercised by those authorities closest to the citizen (the 'subsidiarity' principle);

  o   changes in the territorial structure of local government should not be possible without the involvement of an independent commission;

  o   local authorities should be able to determine their own political and management structures, without interference from the centre.

- Over time, an independent review of the appropriate division of responsibilities between central and local government should take place, prioritising education, housing, health and social care, land-use planning, community safety, and environmental sustainability.

Local-government finance

- Local authorities should be entitled to adequate financial resources of their own, commensurate with the responsibilities allocated to them, which they should be able to dispose of freely, within the framework of their statutory powers.
- The financial resources of local authorities should be derived from local taxes and charges, over which they have the power to determine the

rate. The only exception should be grants designed to correct the effects of the unequal distribution of sources of local finance, and financial burdens that they support.

- There should be three main constituents of local-government finance: council tax; scope to raise a modest level of income tax; and central-government grant to provide a measure of equalisation to respond to disparities in the revenue – raising capacity of different authorities.

- Business rates should be retained in full by local authorities, but in the form of a component of central grant, distributed in a way that gives upper-tier authorities a larger share of the revenue.

- A range of different appropriate sources of local tax should be identified, and local authorities permitted to utilise whatever mix of such taxes fits their particular circumstances.

- A revaluation of property values should be carried out, and a greater number of (council) tax bands identified, to enhance fairness by increasing the yield from high-value properties, especially in London.

- The use of specific grants should be restricted to areas of activity in which central government wishes to encourage local authorities to take action, without a justification for requiring them to do so.

- For the purpose of borrowing for capital investment, local authorities should have access to the national capital market.

- The capping of local sources of finance, whether directly or by enforced referenda, should be discontinued.

Local democratic arrangements

- Any local authority wishing to introduce an elected mayor should have the choice of electing one from within the council as an alternative to direct election, without the need to hold a referendum.

- The constituency/ward-based system of local elections should be retained, but a 'compensatory top-up mechanism' should be introduced to reduce the possibility of 'one-party states' coming into being as a result of gaining 50 per cent or more of the overall vote.

- Single member wards should become normal practice. Ward size should ideally be about 5000 in population, except in large counties and cities such as Kent and Birmingham, where a larger ward size may be appropriate.

- The choice of frequency of local elections (every four years, or three years out of four) should remain with local authorities themselves.

Territorial structure

- In the longer term, an independent evidence-based study should be carried out to review the current confusing structure of local government in England, and to make recommendations for change that reflect the constitutional principles set out above. The presumption in favour of unitary authorities should be dropped, and the recent establishment of Combined Authorities open to reconsideration.

All of these proposals would do much to strengthen local government, reverse the 40 years of centralisation, and move towards a better central–local settlement. But they would not in themselves be enough. As we emphasised earlier, formal changes of this nature, important though they are, would be only part of what is required. They would need to be accompanied by a change of attitude and culture within the civil service, not just within the relatively low-status Department of Communities and Local Government, but also encompassing the Treasury, the Home Office, and the Departments of Health and Education, and other departments that have an impact directly or indirectly upon local affairs. The adoption of the changes set out above, and in particular the proposals for constitutional change, should be seen as a signal of the need for radical change in central government, and a rejection of the centralist culture that currently predominates. This change will not be easy to accomplish; the disdain in which local government is held is apparent amongst senior civil servants and most ministers, and their unjustified assumptions about the 'low calibre' of councillors and the inferiority of local-government managers (compared with the civil service) are deep rooted and will not easily be changed. The current state of both local government and central government cannot be justified. A mature democratic country such as England, with a population approaching 60 million, needs a vibrant system of local democracy, in which local authorities are able to make local choices that affect the well-being of their populations, rather than, as at present, act primarily as agents for implementing policies handed down from Westminster. If this book succeeds in increasing awareness of this unacceptable democratic deficit, and motivates people to try to do something about it, it will have achieved its aim. Our failing system of government requires not abolition but radical change.

REFERENCES

Allen, H. J. B. (1990) *Cultivating the Grass Roots: Why Local Government Matters* (The Hague, IULA)

Atkinson, H. and Wilks-Heeg, S. (2000) *Local Government from Thatcher to Blair: The Politics of Creative Autonomy* (Oxford, Wiley)

Bains, M. (Chairperson) (1972) *The New Local Authorities: Management and Structure* (London, HMSO)

Birmingham City Council (2006) *Devolution and Localisation: A Report from Overview and Scrutiny* (Birmingham, Birmingham City Council)

Blair, T. (1998) *Leading the Way: A New Vision for Local Government* (London, IPPR)

Branson, N. (1979) *Poplarism 1919–1925* (London, Lawrence and Wishart)

Brockway, F. (1949) *Bermondsey Story: The Life of Alfred Salter* (London, Allen and Unwin)

Brown, A. (2014) *The Myth of the Strong Leader: Political Leadership in the Modern Age* (London, The Bodley Head)

Chandler, J. (2010) 'A Rationale for Local Government', *Local Government Studies*, 36(1), pp5–20

Chisholm, M. and Leach, S. (2008) *Botched Business: The Damaging Process of Reorganising Local Government 2006–2008* (Coleford, Glous, Douglas McLean Publishing)

Communities and Local Government (CLG) (2011a) *Implementing Self-Financing for Council Housing (Consultation Paper)* (London, CLG)

Communities and Local Government (CLG) (2011b) *Open Public Services* Cmnd 8145 (London, CLG)

Conservative Party (2009) *Control Shift: Returning Power to Local Communities* (Policy Green Paper No 5) (London, Conservative Party)

Copus, C. (2006) 'British Local Government: A Case for a New Constitutional Settlement', *Public Policy and Administration*, 21(2), pp4–21

Copus, C. (2010) 'English Local Government: Neither Local nor Government' in Swianiewicz, P. (2010) *Territorial Consolidation Reforms in Europe* (Budapest, Local Government and Public Service Reform Initiative, Open Society Institute)

Copus, C. (2011) 'English Local Government: Reflecting a Nation's Past or Merely an Administrative Convenience?' in Aughey, A. and Berberich, C. (2011) *These Englands* (Manchester, Manchester University Press)

Copus, C., Sweeting, D. and Wingfield, M. (2013) 'Re-politicising and Re-democratising Local Democracy and the Public Realm: Why We Need Councillors and Councils', *Policy and Politics*, 43, pp389–408

Department for Communities and Local Government (DCLG) (2006) *Strong and Prosperous Communities: The Local Government White Paper* (London, DCLG)

Department of the Environment (DoE) (1979) *Organic Change in Local Government Cmnd 7457* (London, HMSO)

Goss, S. (1988) *Local Labour and Local Government* (Edinburgh, Edinburgh University Press)

Herbert, E. (Chairperson) *Royal Commission on Local Government in Greater London 1957–60, Report Cmnd 1164* (London, HMSO)

House of Commons Communities and Local Government (2016) *Devolution: The Next Five Years and Beyond* (London, The Stationery Office)

Jenkins, S. (1994) *Accountable to None: The Tory Nationalisation of Britain* (London, Penguin)

Jenkins, S. (2004) *Big Bang Localism* (London, Policy Exchange)

Jenkins, S. (2006) *Thatcher and Sons: A Revolution in Three Acts* (London, Allen Lane)

Jenkins, S. (2012) 'This bid to force schools into line will end in failure' (*The Guardian*, 28 November 2012)

Jenkins, S. (2013) 'Unlike most government reforms, the impact of planning change is forever' (*The Guardian*, 27 March 2013)

Jones, G. and Stewart, J. (1983) *The Case for Local Government* (London, Allen and Unwin)

Jones, G. and Stewart, J. (2011) 'Local Government: Past, Present and Future' (Frank Stacey Memorial Lecture) *Public Administration Conference Papers*, September 2011

Jones, G. and Stewart, J. (2016) 'Lessons from Layfield – 40 years on' (*Municipal Journal*, 8 December 2016)

Jones, G. and Travers, T. (1994) *Central Government Perceptions of Local Government* (London, Commission for Local Democracy)

Jones, O. (2014) *The Establishment: And How They Get Away with It* (Harmondsworth, Penguin)

King, A. and Crewe, I. (2016) *The Blunders of Our Governments* (London, Oneworld Publications)

Kings Fund (2015) *Social Care for Older People: Home Truths* (London, Kings Fund)

Layfield Committee (1976) *Report of the Committee into Local Government Finance Cmnd 6543* (London, HMSO)

Leach, S. (2010) 'The Labour Government's Local Government Agenda 1997–2009: The impact on Member–Officer Relationships', *Local Government Studies*, 36(3), pp323–340

Leach, S. and Lowndes, V. (1994) *Fitness for Purpose in the 21st Century* (London, Audit Commission/IDeA)

Leach, S., Hartley, J., Lowndes, V., Wilson, D. and Downe, J. (2005) *Political Leadership in England and Wales* (York, Joseph Rowntree Foundation)

Lindblom, C. (1959) 'The Science of Muddling Through', *Public Administration Review*, 9 (Spring), pp70–88

London Finance Commission (2013) *Raising the Capital: Report of the London Finance Commission* (London, London Finance Commission)

Loughlin, M. (1996) *Legality and Locality: The Role of Law in Central–Local Relations* (Oxford, Oxford University Press)

Loughlin, M., Gelfand, M. and Young, K. (eds) (1985) *Half a Century of Municipal Decline 1935–1985* (London, Allen and Unwin)

Lowndes, V., Pratchett, L. and Stoker, G. (2001) 'Trends in Public Participation: Part One', *Public Administration*, 79(1), pp205–222

Lyons, Sir M. (2007) *Place-shaping: A Shared Ambition for the Future of Local Government, Final Report of the Lyons Enquiry into Local Government* (London, HMSO)

MacFadyen, P. (2014) *Flatpack Democracy: A DIY Guide to Creating Independent Politics* (Bath, Eco-logical Books)

Maud, J. (Chairman) (1967) *Committee on the Management of Local Government. Vol 1 Report* (Norwich, TSO)

Meek, J. (2014) *Private Island: Why Britain Now Belongs to Someone Else* (London, Verso)

O'Hara, M. (2015) *Austerity Bites: A Journey to the Sharp End of the Cuts in the UK* (Bristol, Policy Press)

Osborne, P. (2001) *The Triumph of the Political Class* (London, Pocket Books)

Office of the Deputy Prime Minister (ODPM) (2005) *Vibrant Local Leadership* (London, ODPM)

Planning Advisory Group (1965) *The Future of Development Plans* (London, Ministry of Housing and Local Government)

Redcliffe-Maud, J (Chairperson) (1969) *Royal Commission on Local Government in England 1966–69 Vol 1 Report Cmnd 4040* (London, HMSO)

Roberts, M. (2016) 'Communication Breakdown: Understanding the Role of Policy Narratives in Political Conflict and Consensus', *Critical Policy Studies*, pp1–21 (online)

Seldon, A. and Snowden, P. (2016) *Cameron at 10: The Verdict* (London, William Collins)

Stewart, J. (2000) *The Nature of British Local Government* (Basingstoke, Palgrave)

Toynbee, P. and Walker, D. (2014) *Cameron's Coup: How the Tories took Britain to the Brink* (London, Guardian Books)

Wheatley Lord (Chairperson) (1969) *Royal Commission on Local Government in Scotland, Report, Cmnd 4150* (Edinburgh, HMSO)

Widdicombe, D. (Chairperson) (1986) *Report of the Committee of Inquiry into the Conduct of Local Authority Business, Cmnd 9797* (London, HMSO)

Wilmott, D. and Young, M. (1957) *Family and Kinship in East London* (Harmondsworth, Penguin Classics)

Wilson, D. and Game, C. (2011) *Local Government in the United Kingdom* (5th edition) (Basingstoke, Palgrave Macmillan)

INDEX

 Taylor & Francis eBooks

Helping you to choose the right eBooks for your Library

Add Routledge titles to your library's digital collection today. Taylor and Francis ebooks contains over 50,000 titles in the Humanities, Social Sciences, Behavioural Sciences, Built Environment and Law.

Choose from a range of subject packages or create your own!

Benefits for you

» Free MARC records
» COUNTER-compliant usage statistics
» Flexible purchase and pricing options
» All titles DRM-free.

 REQUEST YOUR FREE INSTITUTIONAL TRIAL TODAY

Free Trials Available
We offer free trials to qualifying academic, corporate and government customers.

Benefits for your user

» Off-site, anytime access via Athens or referring URL
» Print or copy pages or chapters
» Full content search
» Bookmark, highlight and annotate text
» Access to thousands of pages of quality research at the click of a button.

eCollections – Choose from over 30 subject eCollections, including:

Archaeology	Language Learning
Architecture	Law
Asian Studies	Literature
Business & Management	Media & Communication
Classical Studies	Middle East Studies
Construction	Music
Creative & Media Arts	Philosophy
Criminology & Criminal Justice	Planning
Economics	Politics
Education	Psychology & Mental Health
Energy	Religion
Engineering	Security
English Language & Linguistics	Social Work
Environment & Sustainability	Sociology
Geography	Sport
Health Studies	Theatre & Performance
History	Tourism, Hospitality & Events

For more information, pricing enquiries or to order a free trial, please contact your local sales team:
www.tandfebooks.com/page/sales

 Routledge
Taylor & Francis Group

The home of
Routledge books

www.tandfebooks.com